OCCUPY MOVEMENT
and the DICTATORSHIP
of the PROLETARIAT

SECOND EDITION

OCCUPY MOVEMENT
and the DICTATORSHIP
of the PROLETARIAT

SECOND EDITION

GERALD McISAAC

Printed in the United States of America

ISBN: 978-1-959483-33-5 (sc)
ISBN: 978-1-959483-34-2 (hc)
ISBN: 978-1-959483-35-9 (e)

Library of Congress Control Number: Pending

History
2023.02.13

CONTENTS

PREFACE

Here in North America, on 17 September, 2011, in New York City, an Occupy Wall Street protest is widely regarded as the beginning of the protest movement in North America.

It should be noted that Wall Street is the financial headquarters of the United States.

The social scientists say "this is part of an international protest movement against social and economic inequality. Among the primary concerns are the manner in which the large corporations and the global financial system control the world in a way that disproportionately benefits a minority, undermines democracy, and is unstable. It has been referred to as the global justice movement."

So much for the kind words of the social scientists, those whom, for the most part, bend over backwards in an effort not to offend the capitalists, the billionaires, the bourgeoisie.

In fact, this is just a continuation of the revolution which first broke out in Tunisia in January of that year.

The people who have taken to the streets are a mixture of working class, technically referred to as proletarians, and middle class, technically referred to as petty bourgeois. At the time of the protests, they tended to refer to themselves as the "99 percent", as opposed to the tiny minority of extremely wealthy people, the "1 percent", by whom they meant the monopoly capitalist class, the billionaires, the bourgeoisie. The fact that such protesters no longer refer to themselves as the "99 percent" is a step in the right direction. Nor do they refer to the bourgeoisie as the "1 percent". It indicates an instinctive, growing awareness of the existence of classes.

I should mention that, for the purposes of this article, I refer to members of the working class, the proletariat, as common people, or members of the public, because that is the way they refer to themselves. The middle class people, the petty bourgeois, the small business owners, I also consider to be working people. Even though they are small time capitalists, they are being driven out of business by the monopolies, forced into the ranks of the proletariat. They are the natural and desirable allies of the proletariat.

The monopoly capitalists, or billionaires, the bourgeoisie, I refer to simply as capitalists. They are the class enemies of the working people.

Further, I refer to the United States as America, and to the people who live there, as Americans. I do this out of respect for those people, as that is the way in which they refer to themselves.

For the benefit of the countless working people, those who are just now becoming politically active, various technical terms are explained. Those who are familiar with those terms may find that tiresome, but it cannot be helped. The "new comers" have to be "brought up to speed".

Most members of the public are quite confused by this spontaneous uprising. For that matter, the people who have taken to the streets are also quite confused. By contrast, the capitalists are supremely well aware that this is just the beginning, the violent outbreak of class warfare. They are determined to confuse the issue as best they can.

It is the purpose of this book to clarify the situation.

The fact is that knowledge is power, and it is important for us, the working people, to educate ourselves. We have got to understand that which is happening. For that reason, it is necessary to employ scientific terms with which most people may not be familiar. We will do our best to explain these terms and hope the reader will bear with us.

It is further a fact that society develops according to certain laws, and it is best to become familiar with those laws.

Such uprisings have happened before, on numerous occasions, and all follow a similar pattern. We can learn from the mistakes of the past, or we can repeat such mistakes.

With that in mind, we have to first examine our history, and by that I mean not just the history of class struggle here in North America, but class struggle around the world. Our history has been robbed from us! We must first determine from where we came, in order to determine just where we are going.

Even though we try to explain this movement from a scientific perspective, there are references to God. For this I make no apologies. The spontaneous movement which is sweeping across the world can only be described as an Act of God.

As for those who choose not to believe in God, I can only say that I respect your belief, and can further suggest that you read it as Higher Power, HP.

In this book, you will find numerous redundancies, and in fact I have deliberately used the scientific name followed by the common names. This is to impress upon people the importance of learning the correct scientific terms.

Those who are aware of these scientific term may find this to be tiresome. Bear in mind that the mass movement is

GERALD McISAAC

growing much stronger. Ever more people, those who were formerly apathetic, are now becoming politically active. It is necessary to raise their level of awareness.

We can start by saying that those who are variously referred to as "working class", "blue collar", "common people", "rank and file", or "members of the public", and who were taking part in the Occupy Movement, were either working class, proletarians, or middle class, petty bourgeois. A proletarian is someone who works for wages, as that person has nothing to sell but his, or her, labor power. The small business owners, or middle class, petty bourgeois, are small time capitalists, but are being driven out of business. We have a common enemy.

By contrast, those who are variously referred to as "capitalists", "entrepreneurs", "business people", "corporate and banking executives", "billionaires", are members of a different class of people, and the scientific term for those people is bourgeoisie. They were formerly referred to as the "1 percent". A capitalist is someone who lives off the labor of others, mainly the working class, the proletarians.

These scientific terms we will explain in greater detail later. For now, suffice it to mention that our interests are diametrically opposed, which is to say, that which is in the best interest of one class, is in the worst interest of the other class.

Perhaps we can also explain such political terms as Left, Right and Centre.

The terms first appeared in France during the revolution of 1789. The members of the National Assembly were literally divided, with supporters of the king sitting to the right of the president, while those who supported the revolution were sitting to his left.

To this day, the Left is referred to as the party of the labour movement, or the working class, and the Right is referred to as the party of "law and order", or the capitalist class, the bourgeoisie. Those who straddle the fence are referred to as Centrists or Moderates, those who vacillate between the Right and the Left, between the capitalists and the workers, depending upon just who appears to be winning the class war at any given time.

While these terms are very general, rather vague, it is generally understood that the Left includes people who support various mass movements, including, but not limited to, the Occupy Movement. These people tend to be working class, proletarians as well as middle class. By contrast, the Right tends to refer to people who support the capitalists, the billionaires, which include the fascists, anarchists, monarchists and reactionaries, among others.

In the spirit of explaining those terms, we should mention that a reactionary is someone who opposes political or social change. Such people want everything to stay precisely the way it is.

CHAPTER 1
Origin of Classes

It may come as a bit of a surprise to most people, to find that classes did not always exist. In fact, for thousands of years, in an age which is commonly referred to as the "stone age", everyone worked together on an equal basis. They had to cooperate, as all were members of a hunting - gathering society. Each day, the food and all other necessities of life had to be gathered or killed. Of necessity, these people were nomads, following the herds, because if they stayed in any one location for too long, they would quickly exhaust their food supply.

As a result of this, each group of people, commonly referred to as bands, had to be rather small, while the area they occupied had to be very large. If there were too many people in a band, then the amount of food that could be gathered or killed was not sufficient to feed everyone. Such a band of course had to split, and the new band had to stake out their own territory,

There was never a surplus, and everyone had to pull their own weight. The survival of the band depended on that. This is not to say that peace and harmony reigned supreme, but it is fair to say that anyone who refused to cooperate and do his share of the work, was kicked out of the band.

This almost always amounted to a death sentence, as an individual had almost no chance of survival under those conditions.

Our ancestors were not top predators, as we are now, but prey animals, and the job of the man was not just to kill the game which our ancestors ate, but also to defend the women and children from predators such as bears and sabre toothed cats, among others. That included any strangers, as all strangers were considered enemies. He was required to keep his weapons close to hand, and when necessary to lay down his life for the band. This left the women to do all the work involved in gathering food, butchering the animals the men killed, as well as raising the children. The life of women in the stone age was one of non-stop work, but then such women were highly respected.

Under such conditions, there was very little leisure time and very little contact between bands of people.

The fact that we exist today is proof that they succeeded, against all the odds, in a world of huge predators. No doubt life was short and brutal.

This lack of leisure time and isolation of bands of people also meant that new ideas were few and far between, and generally short lived. People who are constantly scanning the horizon for predators do not have a great deal of time to consider a new and better way of doing things. Those who did come up with a better invention, such as an improved flint knife, may not have been able to pass on that knowledge, if only because they were soon killed, or unable to make contact with another band.

So inventions, or "improvements in technology", as we refer to them today, were scarce but they did happen. In various parts of the world, stone age people slowly progressed with various inventions, which include the use of fire, weaving baskets, placing wooden handles on knives, spear throwers, bow and arrow, and at a later time, pottery.

The bow and arrow was one of the greatest inventions, a decisive weapon for its time, as it allowed people to kill big game and the hunters were better able to protect the women and children. Of course, those same hunters very quickly learned that it was also very handy for killing other people.

Around the world, over a period of many thousands of years, stone age people progressed through the various stages, and created the same inventions, which lead to civilization.

One of the most important inventions, was the cultivation of crops. Almost certainly, a genius of a young woman was the first to get the idea of scratching up some soil and planting some seeds in the ground. The results were astounding.

Almost immediately, numerous people followed her example and began to cultivate crops. A rather small plot of land could grow a very large amount of food, and as people were no longer required to travel far and wide in search of edible plants and animals, they subsequently began to settle down in villages, at first very crude dwellings, but then they grew and became more elaborate.

It was not just plants that were domesticated and harvested.

In particular, the people of the Eastern Hemisphere were fortunate to be blessed with various animals which were suitable for domestication, such as horses, cattle, donkeys, buffalo, pigs, sheep, goats, chickens and ducks. It was found that once these animals were tamed, they produced food such as milk and cream, milk products such as cheese, wool and hides for clothing, eggs and feathers, as well as offspring once a year.

Animals are similar to people in that they require no great motivation to reproduce.

As a result of this, for the first time in history, people had a surplus. The man was no longer required to hunt every day, as with a minimum of supervision, the livestock reproduced. Hunting, formerly a necessity, now became a luxury, a sport, as it is today.

The man, as the head of the family, claimed these herds as his own, and he now had free time on his hands. Women also benefitted from this new found wealth, but had no part in its ownership.

Rather than sit around and count his blessings, the man decided to enlarge his blessings. With his new found wealth, mainly in the form of domesticated animals, he was able to gather some friends and with the promise of booty, set off to separate his neighbors from their hard earned wealth. If nothing else, he could at least separate them from their freedom, and he did. As a result of this, classes came into existence. The people who were owned became slaves, the exploited, while the people who owned these people became slave owners, the exploiters.

At the risk of being accused of pointing out the obvious, I will mention that it was in the interests of the slave owners to make sure that the slaves worked as hard as possible, while at the same time giving them as little as possible in the way of food, clothing and shelter. At the same time, it was in the interests of the slaves to work as little as possible, especially as the reward for hard work was more hard work. In scientific jargon, we say the interests of the two classes are diametrically opposed. This is just another way of saying that the best interest of one is in the worst interest of the other.

At the dawn of civilization, with the first surplus of goods, classes appeared as people began to enslave people, an age which the scientists refer to as the age of "classical slavery", and it lasted for hundreds of years. The slave owners regarded his slaves as livestock, no different from his other animals, aside from the fact that they were able to speak. The slaves were bred, just as the rest of the animals were bred.

Also in scientific terms, we can say that a class cannot exist in isolation. In fact, a class can exist only with its antipode, which is to say, the class opposite to itself. A class of slave owners can exist only with a class of slaves, a class of nobility can exist only with a class of commoners, and in modern terms, a class of capitalists, or bourgeoisie, can exist only with a corresponding class of workers, or proletarians. We can further say, that which is in the best interests of one class, is absolutely in the worst interests of the other class, or that the class interests are diametrically opposed. This was true in the time of slavery, and it is just as true today. We refer to this as class struggle, or more accurately, class warfare.

The point we are trying to make is that ever since classes first came into existence, the classes have been in competition with each other. The form of the struggle has changed as classes have changed, but only the form. Our interests remain diametrically opposed.

In modern day terms, we can say that the interests of the capitalists, the bourgeoisie, are diametrically opposed to the interests of the workers, the proletarians.

To return to the age of the dawn of civilization, this created a little problem for the slave owners, in that the slaves were reluctant to accept their new lot in life. Rather than resign themselves to a life of perpetual labor without pay or even hope of anything better, they tended to rebel. The slave owners regarded this as the based ingratitude, as the owners were careful to feed them just enough to keep them alive and working, as well as reproducing. Clearly something had to be done to keep the slaves in their place, and something was done. A state apparatus was formed.

At first, this took the form of armed men who made sure the slaves did not rebel. Any such act was crushed with the utmost brutality. A system of torture and death was devised which was as cruel and prolonged as possible. The Romans perfected this fine art of execution with crucifixion, whereby an individual could hang on the cross for a week or more before dying. This slow death was not so much punishment for rebelling as it was a warning to others who might consider such a course of action.

Later, as times changed, this state apparatus was used to keep other, so called "lower classes", in line. At no time did the state disappear and at no time did the state become impartial. The state always has been, and is now, a public force that the ruling class uses to crush the resistance of the lower classes. Over the years, the state apparatus has changed in form, but only in form. At no time has it changed its character. It always has been, and remains, a force to ensure the ruling class remains in power.

In modern times, it is composed of the military, police, jails, prisons and various coercive institutions. It is the form of the state apparatus, which the capitalists, the bourgeoisie, has set up in order to keep the workers, the proletarians, under control.

CHAPTER 2
Classical Slavery and the Feudal System

The country of Greece provides us with a very clear cut example of the earliest result of class struggle.

With the dawn of civilization and the subsequent creation of classes, an era appeared which is known as the "age of antiquity" or "classical slavery". It was not only slavery which was invented but also money in the form of metallic currency, the minted coin. Land also became private property and the mortgage was invented. Those who worked the land, the peasants, had to pay very high interest rates to the landlords. These people were allowed to keep only a small fraction, perhaps ten percent, of the crops they grew. The remainder went towards rent. If that did not cover the payments on the mortgage, then the people were forced to sell their children into slavery. If the bloodsucker of a landlord was still not satisfied, then the people who worked the land were also sold into slavery.

As can be imagined, the situation arose where a few people became very rich, at least according to the standards of the day, while the vast majority of people were impoverished, if not outright enslaved.

In modern terms, we would say that the economy was in a shambles, just as we can say that the economies of most countries of the world today are in a shambles.

The situation in Greece at that time could not go on and the precise details are not clear, but the fact is that a revolution happened. It was the first political revolution, at least in the western world, in the year 594 BCE (Before the Common Era) but it was certainly not the last. Credit for this revolution is given to an individual by the name of Solon, and while he no doubt was happy to take the credit, the revolution was almost certainly the result of a mass movement by the people of Greece. Solon just happened to be the leader at that time.

As a result of this revolution, Greek slaves were released from slavery and the citizens who had fled or been sold abroad were brought back. The mortgages were declared null and void, and the people who worked the land were allowed to own the land they worked.

It is significant that the Greek slaves were emancipated, but through no effort on their part. Slaves are not capable of mounting an independent revolt to secure their emancipation. The conditions which exist, under slavery, simply do not allow for such an event.

It is clear that Solon was not opposed to slavery, but to the slavery of the citizens of Greece. The slaves who were not Greeks, were not emancipated. He was certainly a patriotic citizen and realized that the enslavement of Greek citizens was destroying the country.

The people who owned all the slaves and mortgages were the people who had the most money, the landlords. These were the modern day equivalent of the capitalists, the billionaires, the bourgeoisie. Their property was under attack and they were not at all anxious to part with their hard stolen wealth. But part with it they did, as they were persuaded with swords and spears. These people howled that they were being robbed, and their property was being violated. True! Their property was violated! The property of the tiny minority, the landlords and slave owners, was violated so as to benefit the vast majority, the Greek slaves, peasants and working people, the modern day equivalent of the working class.

To put it in modern day terms, this gave a huge "boost to the economy", and the country of Greece was saved.

Since that time, there have been numerous revolutions, and all have followed a similar pattern. Property of one class, the ruling class, the tiny minority, has been violated in order to protect another kind of property, the property of the vast majority. One cannot be protected without violating the other. This is to say that the property of the tiny minority, the capitalists, the bourgeoisie, has to be violated in order to protect the property of the vast majority, the working class, the proletariat.

May the billionaires take notice: very soon, your property, the property of the tiny minority, will be violated in order to protect the property of the vast majority, the working class.

To return to the time of ancient Greece, we stress that this did not abolish slavery, it merely abolished the slavery of Greek citizens.

The institution of slavery was completely accepted and was well entrenched. Of course the slaves resisted and there were occasional slave rebellions, but none of them was successful. Such revolts were suppressed, generally with the utmost brutality.

The Roman Empire provides us with a very clear cut example of this, as slavery in the empire existed for 500 years, from 150 BCE to 350 CE. At no point in the history of the Roman Empire did the slaves mount a successful revolt. We stress that even though the slaves resisted, conditions did not allow for success.

Aside from slaves and slave owners, there were free people, but they could not compete with slave labor, and generally had no desire to do so. For the most part, they merely became "social scrap", a great mass of unemployed, a burden on society.

The fact is that classical slavery gradually died out, but not because the slave owners considered anything immoral in the fact that they owned slaves, but simply because it was inefficient. The slaves learned very quickly that hard work did not result in any improvement in their quality of life. If anything, it was just the opposite. The harder the slave worked, the harder he was expected to work. As a result of this, slaves became experts at doing practically nothing.

Of course, the slave owners saw this from a different point of view. They just thought the slaves were lazy. They tried to motivate their slaves to work harder, generally with the persuasion of a whip, but such methods were generally ineffective.

After a period of centuries, classical slavery died out.

At the same time that classical slavery died out, classes did not die out with them. They merely evolved. Instead of having a very clear distinction of two classes, slaves and slave owners, it gave way to a more elaborate system, called feudalism.

This is commonly referred to as the "middle ages".

We should add that there were a few former slaves who managed to amass great wealth, at least by the standards of the time, and set themselves up as kings, usually of rather small areas. Then it was a simple matter of creating larger areas, either by conquest or by creating political alliances, frequently by marriage.

These descendants of slaves, newly created kings, set themselves up as nobles who claimed to be far superior to the common people. In fact, our current crop of European inbred nobility still make that claim. They carefully ignore the fact that their ancestors were slaves.

At that time, the king gave grants of land to his most important noblemen, and in return each noble pledged an oath of loyalty to the king and promised to provide the king with soldiers in time of war. The nobles then frequently divided their land between lower lords, called knights, who then became the vassals of the lords. Then there was a very complicated arrangement of tradesmen. The members of the clergy were also very powerful, and within each group, there was a strict pecking order, with of course the king at the top.

At the very bottom rung of the social ladder were the peasants, also called serfs, who had to work the land and pay the lord a portion of their crop each year. They had almost no rights and could be sold with the land. In fact, they were not much better off than slaves. They were expected to work for the lord and act as foot soldiers in time of war. In turn, the lord promised to protect them, although he did not promise to protect them from himself.

The feudal system was a very complicated system, with a strict hierarchy, very inefficient, but it lasted for centuries, with the king at the head.

Of course, to this day the nobility has been trying to keep the power within the family, mainly by marrying each other. As can be expected, they have all come to grief over this.

From bitter experience, the nobles are aware that inbreeding is not healthy. This is just as true for people as it is for animals.

One of the most striking examples of this is within the House of Hapsburg. Those fools intermarried often and gave birth to a great many halfwits. The dynasty mercifully came to an end with Charles II of Spain, who was incapable of reproducing.

After centuries of copulating with each other and giving birth to physically and intellectually challenged offspring, even the nobility is now facing the fact that such acts are not healthy. In the face of possible extinction of their blood line, they are taking the extreme measure of forcing their offspring to marry "commoners", as they refer to us. The fact that the younger nobles are now being forced to marry us, the common people, does not mean that they find us any less contemptible. They just have no choice in the matter.

A fine example of this is the current Queen of England, who is rather closely related to her husband. These cousins are both descended from Queen Victoria of Britain and Christian IX of Denmark. It should come as no great surprise to anyone that their offspring are widely regarded as simple souls, not overly bright.

If there is anything worse, from the viewpoint of the nobility, of not being able to give birth to an heir to the throne, it is giving birth to such an heir, and wishing you had not.

That is the current predicament of the British nobility.

This arrogance of the nobility, which is a natural result of having wealth and power, is also characteristic of the bourgeoisie. It is not by chance that the American bourgeoisie is commonly referred to as the "new nobility"!

Here in North America, many such families first earned their fortune from the slave trade. They became rich from selling people. Others found acts of piracy to be most profitable. Still others, and one family in particular, made their fortune in the days of prohibition by selling illegal alcohol. It was not just Al Capone and the Mob who profited from prohibition! This particular family has used that wealth to become very active in American politics. They choose not to brag about the fact that they are highly successful bootleggers.

To return to the feudal system, it persisted for centuries, and during that time the peasants supplied the lords with crops and manpower, but then there were certain items which only the tradesmen could provide, such as weapons and armour, and the tradesmen lived in town.

The lords also wanted luxury items such as silk and spices, and these were provided by a class of merchants who also lived in town. These merchants were referred to as burghers, and trade was their specialty. From these rather humble beginnings, they became an extremely powerful class, with the advent of the industrial revolution.

The burghers did not concern themselves with production but merely with the exchange of products. They set themselves up as the middle men between the producers and the consumers and exploited both. Claiming to be the most useful class of the population, while in fact providing a most insignificant service, they skimmed the cream from producer and consumer alike, and amassed a vast fortune.

This placed them in a fine position to take advantage of the opportunities presented by the industrial revolution.

CHAPTER 3
Revolution:
Industrial and Social

The industrial revolution began in Great Britain, for reasons which do not directly concern us, within the years 1760-1840, and quickly spread to Europe and North America.

Up until the time of the industrial revolution, all manufactured goods had to be produced by hand. Everything from dishes to diapers, muskets to candles, were all made by hand. The process was tedious and time consuming, and today, in the twenty first century, we tend to lose sight of that fact.

The burghers had money and saw the potential of making far more money. The only thing they had to do was build factories, mills, mines and other structures referred to as the "means of production", as well as take control of the banks and financial institutions, railroads and shipping lines, foundries and electric plants, and run them for a profit.

This is precisely what they did, and in this, they were supremely successful.

In fact, they took control of almost everything of any considerable value, and in the process became supremely rich

and powerful, transformed from a rather small, unimportant
class, to a very powerful class of people we are cursed with
today, the capitalists, the "bourgeoisie".

We say powerful, because along with wealth, comes
power.

Almost overnight, these factories were producing vast
quantities of products. They were also able to produce
steam powered boats, ships and railways, which are used
to transport the finished goods to market. The burgers also
seized control of the banks and financial institutions, and
ended up in control of the economies of the country.

Historians are agreed that the industrial revolution was
the most important event in the history of humanity since the
domestication of plants and animals. In this, the historians
are absolutely correct.

From the word burgher, they became known as the
bourgeois. The small time business people became known
as middle class, or petty bourgeois, as petty means small,
while the super-rich became known as the bourgeoisie, the
capitalists.

The fact that the industrial revolution has made it possible
to create vast quantities of goods which can benefit the vast
majority of people does not concern them. The only thing
they care about is their profit.

As a result of the industrial revolution, those who had
formerly produced goods by hand could not compete, as
goods which were produced by machine were sold at a far
lower price.

The newly created class, created from the burghers, tend
to not call themselves capitalists. They prefer such terms as
"entrepreneurs" or "business people". They tend to use the

term "free enterprise", as opposed to capitalism, in an attempt to sanitize the stinking mess.

It was the industrial revolution which made possible the transition of the burgers, a rather small unimportant class, to the extremely rich and powerful class of capitalists we have today, the bourgeoisie. But just as every coin has two sides, and in fact one cannot exist without the other, the creation of this new class of burghers also gave birth to a new class of people, called "proletarians", or workers, people who have nothing to sell but their labor power, and of necessity, ended up working for the capitalists.

Faced with ruin and starvation, the peasants and tradesmen moved to the cities in order to secure jobs in the factories. In the process, they were transformed from peasants and tradesmen to workers, wage - slaves or proletarians.

The conditions created by the industrial revolution was in direct opposition to the old feudal system, which had been in place for centuries. In contrast to the feudal system, with its complicated system of various classes and various levels within classes, we now have simplified class antagonisms, mainly workers and capitalists.

As an immediate result of this vast increase in production, the stage was set for countless millions of people to benefit from this great surplus of goods, and in fact that is still the case. The potential is there, but it has yet to be realized. Rest assured, as long as the capitalists, the bourgeoisie, remain in power, that potential will never be realized.

That is without doubt the way it is today, and equally without doubt, that is not acceptable. It has got to change. The working class has got to overthrow the capitalists, the bourgeoisie, seize political power, destroy the existing state apparatus, and set up a new proletarian state apparatus, in the form of the Dictatorship of the Proletariat. This new state apparatus is necessary to crush the desperate and determined resistance of the capitalists, as they make every attempt to restore their "paradise lost".

Now it is a matter of persuading them to part with their hard stolen wealth.

Of course we are talking about socialism, and making the transition from capitalism to socialism. This will require a revolution, just as a revolution was required to persuade the French nobility to part with their wealth and power.

It should be noted that the industrial revolution did more than destroy the peasantry and tradesmen. True, they were transformed into proletarians. Yet it also destroyed the class of people who depended on the peasants and tradesmen, the landlords and nobles.

This is not to say that the rising class of bourgeois had any desire to destroy the nobility! On the contrary, the bourgeois were anxious to join the nobility! Despite their finest efforts, the bourgeois succeeded in destroying the nobility! The ruling class of nobility was overthrown!

Of course, in certain parts of the world, particularly in Europe, we still have the remnants of the nobility. While previously their power was almost absolute, now it is very slight.

The point being, that the industrial revolution gave birth to productive forces, which are beyond the control of mortal man.

Now that the revolutionary motion has spread across the world, it should help to know what to expect. We can start with the first revolution of the industrial era.

These revolutionary forces very quickly flexed their muscles, although not in Great Britain, as might be expected, but in France.

The French Revolution of 1789-1799 was the first of the modern age. All further revolutionary movements can look back on this as their predecessor, and in fact we can learn from this revolution.

At that time, in France, as well as in most of Europe, the monarchy, also called the nobility, had almost unlimited power. The king was referred to as the monarch, while his relatives were referred to as the nobility. Further, it was the opinion of the nobility, as it is today, that the "lower classes" should know their place. They think it is not the place of the lower classes to challenge their "betters", as the upper classes think of themselves.

The king and the other nobles were part of a class referred to as the "first estate", while the members of the clergy, who were at that time a very powerful force, were referred to as the "second estate". All common people were lumped together under the heading of the "third estate".

These terms were first coined in the French Revolution, and gave rise to a most unusual alliance. The wealthy class of merchants and manufacturers, capitalists or bourgeois, resented their exclusion from political power. So an alliance was formed, between the capitalists, the peasants, and the growing class of working people, the proletarians.

The peasants and workers were also dissatisfied with their lot in life, due in no small part to the revolutionary ideas of "liberty, equality and fraternity".

The fact of the matter, is that there was a time when the bourgeoisie played a revolutionary role! They even formed an alliance with the peasants and proletariat! That was not the only time, I might add. But more on that, later in this article.

To the absolute shock and horror of the nobility, these changing conditions gave rise to social revolution. This meant that the third estate, which is to say the bourgeoisie, along with the workers and peasants, rose up and challenged the authority of the nobility!

To add to the confusion, at that time in Europe, during the French Revolution, there was a group of people, called intellectuals or the "intelligentsia", who considered themselves the smartest people in the world.

These are more terms which the working class must learn, as an intellectual is someone with a rather considerable amount of education. As a group they refer to themselves as members of the intelligentsia.

They were convinced that the "age of reason", otherwise known as the "age of enlightenment", was upon us. They were further convinced that the smartest people in the world, by whom they of course meant themselves, could control a business or even a country. The success or failure of such an undertaking was entirely in the hands of the leaders. In short, smart people make history. Or so they thought.

The intellectuals were successful in persuading the nobility that as long as very intelligent people, such as themselves, were in charge of key government positions, then no one had anything to fear. The fate of the country was in good hands. On this point the intellectuals had no doubt, and on this point they could not possibly have been more mistaken.

We stress the fact that the members of these various classes, proletarians, peasants and bourgeoisie, were not aware of that which they were doing. They rose up spontaneously, or to put it in scientific terms, they were not "conscious of their actions". This in no way changes the fact that they made history, and proves once and for all that the members of the public, working class people make history, not smart men with bright ideas. Not only was the nobility overthrown, but the Age of Reason was proven to be a fable.

As remarkable as it may sound today, the French nobility was not the slightest bit concerned with the revolution that was about to overthrow them. In fact, the revolutionary motion built up for years, and yet the nobles were only vaguely aware of it.

It is characteristic of the nobility that they have an extremely high opinion of themselves and that their biggest problem is boredom. As a result of this, they try to relieve their boredom with parties. At no point did the French nobility concern themselves with the suffering of the common people. Even when the revolution was raging all around them, the nobles were concerned only with squabbling among themselves and their parties. In fact, this is characteristic of the ruling classes in almost all countries.

The French revolution of 1789 shocked the intellectuals to the very core of their being, especially because it was successful. Absolutely no intellectual thought the revolution was a good idea. Not one of them gave it their blessings. In fact, none of them even thought it was possible. No one gave it a second thought until it was happening, and then it was a little late. They were all absolutely dumb founded when the lower classes, the third estate, the bourgeoisie with the workers and peasants, rose up and challenged the upper classes, the nobility!

The people who were most surprised by the revolution, were the nobility. It just never occurred to them that the

common people would rise up and challenge them! Still less
did it cross their mind that the people would succeed!

It was a spontaneous uprising, and no one understood
just what was happening. The intellectuals were convinced
that such an uprising was simply not possible. It was also
their understanding that all movements need a leader, and
of course there were no leaders, although leaders did emerge.

In all fairness to the nobility, they were assisted in this
fatal delusion by their flunkies. The commoners, who worked
for the nobility, were careful to tell their masters precisely that
which they wanted to hear. In modern terms, these people
are commonly referred to as class traitors, flunkies, lapdogs,
or belly crawling boot lickers.

Finally, the day arrived when the revolutionaries were
breaking down the doors of the castles of the nobility, and
the nobles were astounded to find that their "subjects" were
revolting and further, that their flunkies had deserted them.

Of course, it was a full scale revolution and the property
of the nobility was violated. Not only did their property
suffer, but most of the nobility paid for their indifference to
the suffering of the common people, by being separated from
their heads.

The flunkies of the nobility had no loyalty to their
masters and merely worked for them as long as it was safe and
profitable to do so. As soon as their lives were in danger, they
merely joined the revolutionaries. This is the characteristic
response of flunkies in all subsequent revolutions.

As for the intellectuals, they remained cowering behind
closed doors, in a state of deep mental depression. It was not
just their world, the physical world which was collapsing
all around them, but also everything they had believed in,

everything they had stood for, the work to which they had devoted their lives, all was now null and void.

The intellectuals who were capable of honesty, and such were few and far between, had to face the sickening fact that the people were making history.

People truly get into motion, by the millions, not aware of that which they are doing. This in no way changes the fact that by their actions, they are making history. As Marxists phrase it, "the masses are the makers of history." Those of us who believe in God, refer to this as a modern day miracle, an Act of God.

Yet to this day, the fable persists that smart people make history.

That is precisely the problem which must be addressed. The people who were formerly taking part in the Occupy Movement, and currently taking part in other Movements, are not aware of that fact. Their "level of consciousness" must be raised, to put it in scientific terms. They must be made aware that they are members of a revolutionary class, a class of proletarians. As such, they are destined to overthrow the capitalist class, the bourgeoisie, and establish the Dictatorship of the Proletariat. Now we have to make them aware of this fact.

As mentioned previously, the interests of the capitalists are diametrically opposed to the interests of the workers. But at the time of the revolution in France, they had a common enemy. The nobility.

Of course, now that the nobility has long since been overthrown, the alliance is over, and capitalist and workers in France are once again, mortal enemies.

At least here in North America, where we have no nobility, there is no chance of such an alliance, and it is open class warfare between the between capitalists and workers, between bourgeoisie and proletarians.

CHAPTER 4
Marx and Engels: Scientific Socialism and the Communist Manifesto

Karl Marx and Friedrich Engels were German philosophers and the founders of scientific socialism, both of whom lived and worked in the mid to late nineteenth century. They were also members of the bourgeois intelligentsia, and could have lived a life of relative comfort and luxury, as members of the middle class. They chose instead to work in the service of the "common people", which is to say the peasants and growing class of workers, the proletarians. In this service, they did a magnificent job, and in consequence, lived a life of relative poverty.

It was Marx and Engels who first put socialism on a scientific basis and proved that it is necessary and inevitable, from the point of view of the "materialist conception of history".

This stands in sharp contrast to the utopian vision of socialism, those who think that it is merely a good idea.

Engels drew a clear distinction between the socialism of the idealists, called "utopian socialism", and the socialism of the scientists, called quite reasonably, "Scientific Socialism", in his book, Socialism: Utopian and Scientific.

No doubt most people have no problem imagining a society being transformed by machines which can perform the work of many people. Those same people may find the idea that this can change the way people think, change their whole outlook on life, as a bit far-fetched.

In fact, it is not at all far-fetched. We have only to examine the history of civilization, starting with slave owning society. It is safe to say that those people had no concept of socialism, just as feudal society was equally clueless. The conditions under which people lived did not allow for such flights of fantasy.

There were people who were capable of wild stretches of imagination, idealists one and all, and many of them were quite brilliant, among them Aristotle, Plato and Socrates, to name a few. Regardless of how brilliant they were, none of them could conceive of anything outside of their immediate circumstances. The conditions of life did not allow for this. None of those brilliant idealists had any concept of socialism.

The Industrial Revolution created whole new conditions, destroyed some old classes and created new classes, and at the same time destroyed some old ideas while creating new ones. One of these new ideas was that of socialism. As production was socialized, and further, as production is basic to the survival of people, it stood to reason that society should also be socialized. Or so thought the idealists of the time.

They imagined a kingdom of reason and eternal justice, a paradise devoid of class distinctions, a society in which capitalists and workers could live together in peace and harmony, all striving for the common good.

In fact, several attempts were made to set up just such an ideal social society.

In Europe, the capitalists Robert Owen and Charles Fournier, each made a supreme effort. In each case, they failed.

The fact is that classes exist, and our interests are diametrically opposed. No amount of effort on the part of any idealist can change that.

By contrast, it was Marx and Engels who put socialism on a scientific basis. They proved that it is a historical necessity, a natural transition. Just as classical slavery gave way to feudalism, and feudalism in turn gave way to capitalism, so too capitalism must surely give way to socialism.

This is called the "materialist conception of history".

We should also draw a clear distinction between the scientific meaning of materialism, and materialism as many working people understand it.

True, there are material goods such as cars, boats, jewelry and art work, and there are people who love to collect them. Yet to refer to these people as materialists is incorrect, from a scientific point of view. It is more accurate to refer to them as hoarders.

The scientific definition of materialism is far different, and was first put forward by Marx and Engels. With that in mind, it is best we go right to the source, and not rely on that which others say.

As Engels pointed out in his book, Socialism: Utopian and Scientific:

"The materialist conception of history starts from the proposition that the production of the means to support human life, next to production, the exchange of things produced, is the basis of all social structure; that in every society that has appeared in history, the manner in which wealth is distributed and society divided into classes or orders is dependent upon what is produced, how it is produced and how the products are exchanged. From this point of view, the final causes of all social changes and political revolutions can be sought not in men's brains, not in man's better insight into eternal truth and justice, but in changes in the modes of production and exchange. They are to be sought not in the philosophy, but in the economics of each particular epoch."

In modern terms, we now have socialized production, in that vast armies of workers toil in the factories and mills, producing vast quantities of goods. Another vast army of workers transports these goods to market. This is what Engels refers to as the "basis of all social change", and clearly, production and transportation is socialized.

Now that the base is socialized, it is just a matter of bringing the superstructure in line, which is to say the political system. As Engels points out, this can only be done through revolution, as the people who own these factories, mills, mines, railroads and such, are about as anxious to part with their hard stolen wealth, as were the slave owners of ancient Greece, to part with their slaves, or about as anxious as the French nobility were to part with their wealth. In other words, not at all.

Just as the Greek slave owners parted with their slaves, and just as the French nobility parted with their wealth, so too the capitalists, the bourgeoisie, will part with their wealth, however reluctantly. Just as the ruling classes of yesteryear were persuaded with swords and spears, and later with muskets and bayonets, so too the ruling class of today, the capitalists, the bourgeoisie, will receive proper motivation from the working class, the proletarians. The only difference will be the instruments of persuasion. They too will be only too happy to part with their wealth, once the working people get through with them.

The other great discovery of Marx was that of "surplus value", in that the worker adds value to the product produced, the capitalist pays the worker part of this value, and pockets the rest as profit.

It was on the basis of these two great discoveries, the materialist conception of history and that of surplus value, that socialism became a science.

To put it in scientific terms, a materialist explains mans "knowing" by his "being", as opposed to the idealist conception of history, that of mans "being" by his "knowing"

These scientific theories are commonly referred to as Marxist, and encompass an economic theory, a sociological theory, a philosophical method, and a revolutionary view of social change.

They were great revolutionaries, leaders of the oppressed classes. As such, the capitalists subjected them to the most vicious campaign of lies and slander. Their revolutionary theories were mocked and ridiculed, but not discredited, as the capitalists knew that their theories were correct. For their part, the bourgeoisie would rather crawl on their bellies over broken glass, rather than admit this.

After their deaths, the same people who so passionately hated and slandered them, then claimed to be their most devoted followers. They have written countless books on the subject, in an attempt to pervert and distort its revolutionary soul, to revise the Marxism, to change it into something which is acceptable to the bourgeoisie.

Strangely enough, class struggle is acceptable to the bourgeoisie.

As Marx phrased it, in 1852, "Long before me, bourgeois historians had described the historical development of this struggle between the classes, as had bourgeois economists their economic anatomy. My own contribution was 1: To show that the existence of classes is merely bound up with certain historical phases in the development of production; 2; that the class struggle necessarily leads to the Dictatorship of the Proletariat and 3; that this Dictatorship, itself, constitutes no more than a transition to the abolition of all classes and to a classless society".

While class struggle is acceptable to the bourgeoisie, it is revolution and the subsequent Dictatorship of the Proletariat which is absolutely not acceptable. In fact, it is the Dictatorship of the Proletariat which terrifies them, as well it should. After the revolution, after the defeat of the capitalists, then the working class, the proletarians, must crush the bourgeoisie, must exercise Dictatorship over them. We will go into that in more detail later.

We work for the capitalists, as we have no choice in the matter. After all, the capitalists own the factories and all other means of production, and the capitalists expropriate our unpaid labor, in the form of surplus value, which is part of the basis of the materialist conception of scientific socialism. That exploitation, the appropriation of our unpaid labor, has got to stop.

Marx and Engels pointed out that "all past history, with the exception of its primitive stages, was the history of class struggles; that these warring classes of society are always the products of the modes of production and exchange - in a word, of the economic conditions of their time; that the economic structure always furnishes the real basis, starting from which we can alone work out the ultimate explanation of the whole superstructure of juridical and political institutions..."

Their theories stand in sharp contrast to the visions of the idealists, those who think that socialism is just a good idea. That is not the point. Production is basic, is socialized and "forms the economic base", as Marx phrases it, and now it is just a matter of bringing the whole superstructure of judicial and political institutions in line with the base. In other words, we need socialism.

It should be noted that the political institutions are the form of government and the juridical institutions refer to the courts.

I have chosen to refer to their theories of scientific socialism as Marxist, in an attempt to distinguish their theories from those who refer to themselves as Communists, or Socialists, or Social Democrats, or Marxist- Leninist, or Bolsheviks, among other names, but in practice, revise their theories. Do not judge a book by its cover! A true Marxist is one who goes beyond the class struggle and extends this to revolution and the Dictatorship of the Proletariat.

Those who revise the Marxism are merely lapdogs of the capitalists, those who lick the boots of the bourgeoisie, those who think that by diverting all mass movements, they will receive some sort of reward. In fact, the capitalists are very similar to the nobility, in that any flattery or praise they receive, is merely accepted as that which they deserve. In return for this bit of self-degradation, these bootlickers can expect to receive absolutely nothing.

The working people have got to learn to distinguish the true Marxist and those who merely pretend to be Marxists. The phoney Marxists attempt to divert the revolutionary movement onto a course of social and political reform, which is acceptable to the bourgeoisie.

It is for that reason that I have chosen to quote directly from the works of these great revolutionary leaders, and allow the reader to decide.

In 1848, these two published the Manifesto of the Communist Party.

In the introduction, they wrote," A spectre is haunting Europe - the spectre of Communism. All of the powers of old Europe have entered into a holy alliance to exorcise this spectre."

As may be gathered from the statement that "all the old powers of Europe have entered into a holy alliance to exorcise this spectre", it is safe to say that it is something of which the "old powers" do not approve. In fact, this is something which terrifies the capitalists. Anything which terrifies the capitalists certainly demands our immediate, undivided attention. In fact, to say that the capitalists "disapprove" of the theory of scientific socialism, is an understatement. In particular, the expression "Dictatorship of the Proletariat" has, as they phrase it, "negative connotations". This makes them uncomfortable, and it is our duty, the duty of the working people, to relieve them of this discomfort. It is up to us, the working class, to transform that discomfort, that vague sense of unease, into the deepest, darkest, bleakest of all mental depressions. It is the least we can do, and Lord knows, they deserve it.

But then, what is a spectre?

The younger generation of today may find that a bit confusing, as my grandchildren assure me that a spectre is a computer. As this was written long before the computer was invented, I doubt that was the spectre to which Marx and

Engels were referring. Besides, the old powers of Europe do not disapprove of computers.

No, a spectre is something which haunts and terrifies people, such as a spirit, demon or an idea, also called a theory, which keeps people awake nights. It is precisely this theory of scientific socialism, that of revolution and the subsequent Dictatorship of the Proletariat, which terrifies the capitalists.

Since the time that the Communist Manifesto was written, capitalism has spread its tentacles all around the world, and the capitalists in almost all countries of the world are determined to "exorcise this spectre".

In practical terms, that means crushing any and all revolutionary Protest Movements.

They have their work cut out for them.

Chapter 1 of the Communist Manifesto makes it very clear, and since it is so important, I will quote from it at length:

"The history of all hitherto existing society is the history of class struggles.

"Freeman and slave, patrician and plebeian, lord and serf, guild master and journeyman, in a word, oppressor and oppressed, stood in constant opposition to one another, carried on an uninterrupted, now hidden, now open fight, a fight that each time ended, either in a revolutionary reconstitution of society at large, or in the common ruin of the contending classes.

"In the earlier epochs of history, we find almost everywhere a complicated arrangement of society into various orders, a manifold gradation of social rank. In ancient Rome we had patricians, knights, plebeians, slaves; in the Middle Ages, feudal lords, vassals, guild master, journeymen, apprentices, serfs; in almost all of these classes, again, subordinate gradations.

"The modern bourgeois society that has sprouted from the ruins of feudal society has not done away with class antagonisms. It has but established new classes, new conditions of oppression, new forms of struggle in place of the old ones.

"Our epoch, the age of the bourgeoisie, possesses, however, this distinct feature: it has simplified class antagonisms. Society as a whole is more and more split up into two great hostile camps, into two great classes directly facing each other- Bourgeoisie and Proletariat.

"From the serfs of the Middle Ages sprang the chartered burghers of the earliest towns. From these burgesses the first elements of the bourgeoisie were developed...

"The bourgeoisie, historically, has played a most revolutionary part.

"The bourgeoisie, wherever it has got the upper hand, has put an end to all feudal, patriarchal, idyllic relations. It has pitilessly torn asunder the motley feudal ties that bound man to his 'natural superiors', and has left remaining no other nexus between man and man than naked self-interest, then callous 'cash payment'. It has drowned the most heavenly ecstasies of religious fervour, of chivalrous enthusiasm, of philistine sentimentalism, in the icy water of egotistical calculation. It has resolved personal worth into exchange value and in place of the numberless indefeasible chartered freedoms, has set up that single unconscionable freedom - Free Trade. In one word, for exploitation, veiled by religious and political illusions, it has substituted naked, shameless, direct, brutal exploitation.

"The bourgeoisie has stripped of its halo every occupation hitherto honoured and looked up to with reverent awe. It has converted the physician, the lawyer, the priest, the poet,

the man of science, into its paid wage labourers

"The bourgeoisie has torn away from the family its sentimental veil, and has reduced the family relation to a mere money relation.... but not only has the bourgeoisie forged the weapons that will bring death to itself; it has also called into existence the men who are to wield those weapons - the modern working class - the proletarians.

"In proportion as the bourgeoisie, capital, is developed, in the same proportion is the proletariat, the modern working class, developed - a class of labourers who live only so long as they find work, and who find work only so long as their labor increases capital. "These labourers, who must sell themselves piecemeal, are a commodity, like every other article of commerce, and are consequently exposed to all the vicissitudes of competition, to all the fluctuations of the market.

"Of all the classes that stand face to face with the bourgeoisie today, the proletariat alone is really a revolutionary class. The other classes decay and finally disappear in the face of Modern Industry; the proletariat is its special and essential product...

"In depicting the most general phases of the development of the proletariat, we traced the more or less veiled civil war, raging within existing society, up to the point where that war breaks out into open revolution, and where the violent overthrow of the bourgeoisie lays the foundation for the sway of the proletariat."

Without doubt, it is up to us, the working class, the proletariat, to "overthrow the bourgeoisie", to seize political power, and to turn the means of production into state property.

The Communist Manifesto makes it quite clear:

"The first step in the revolution by the working class is to raise the proletariat to the position of ruling class, to win the battle of democracy."

It is significant that the Manifesto refers to the "proletariat raised to the position of ruling class", as merely the "first step" in the revolution, in order to "win the battle of democracy".

The astute reader may find this a bit confusing, as we have all been told that democracy means majority rule, the subordination of the minority to the majority.

In fact, this is not at all the case, as democracy is a state apparatus, one which is set up for the purpose of keeping one class subordinate to another, more powerful class, through the use of violence. As for those who complain that this is not at all democratic at all, we can only respond with one simple question: For which class?

At present, under capitalism, it is the capitalists, the bourgeoisie, an insignificant minority, who are in power, and democracy is only for the capitalists. This is called the dictatorship of the bourgeoisie.

We, the working class, the vast majority, suffer under their rule, the rule of the capitalist class, the bourgeoisie. Millions of working class people, are crushed by a handful of rich, the bourgeoisie.

The democratic rights which we have secured from the capitalists are restricted, cramped, curtailed, mutilated by the conditions of wage slavery. Most members of the working class live in poverty and misery.

Democracy in such conditions, under capitalism, while being crushed by the bourgeoisie, is similar to the democracy of the Athenians, in ancient Greece. It was democracy for a few citizens, men only, the slave owners, and certainly not for the vast majority of people, women, slaves, peasants, poor people. In much the same manner, democracy under capitalism, while the capitalists are in charge, amounts to democracy for the rich, democracy for the billionaires, certainly not democracy for the working class, the proletariat.

So the first step in the revolution, to which the Communist Manifesto refers, that of "raising the proletariat to the position of ruling class", is a matter of overthrowing the capitalists, the bourgeoisie, that insignificant minority currently in charge. At that point, we must first smash the existing state apparatus, which has been set up by the capitalists, for the purpose of crushing the working people. A new, working class state apparatus must be established, in the form of the Dictatorship of the Proletariat. It is this new state apparatus which is necessary to crush the capitalists, the bourgeoisie, to exercise dictatorship over them.

This will result in democracy for the working class, the proletariat, but no democracy at all for the capitalists. The bourgeoisie will suffer under a Dictatorship, our Dictatorship, the Dictatorship of the Proletariat. There is no other way that the Proletariat can maintain state power! The resistance of the capitalists must be crushed! Any attempt on their part to regain political power must be precluded!

The experience of previous revolutions has proven this, beyond any shadow of a doubt!

That point was driven home in 1871, the year the workers in Paris, France, rebelled and established the first working class, socialist government. They referred to it as the "Paris Commune".

This first attempt at a socialist state was brief, lasting only a few weeks, and in fact it failed to achieve its goals, due to a number of reasons. Not the least of which was the fact that the workers failed to smash the existing state machinery. They thought that they could use the existing state apparatus, that which the capitalists had set up. That was a huge mistake!

This is not to say that the Communards can be faulted for this. They merely did not know any better. Now it is up to us to learn from their mistake, not to repeat that mistake!

The lesson was that the state apparatus, which was set up by the capitalists, in order to crush the working class, has to be destroyed.

A new state apparatus must be set up, but one which is Proletarian, not bourgeois, one which can and will be used by the vast majority of the people, the working class, in order to crush the desperate and determined resistance of the capitalists.

Clearly, Marx and Engels regarded this, one of the principle and fundamental lessons of the Paris Commune, of being of such enormous importance that they introduced it as a vital correction in the Communist Manifesto. In the preface to the Manifesto dated 1872, they state:

"...the working class cannot simply lay hold of the ready-made state machinery and yield it for its own purposes."

This is to stress the fact that the existing state apparatus must be smashed. It must be replaced by a new, Proletarian state apparatus, in the form of the Dictatorship of the Proletariat. In no other way, can the Proletariat maintain state power.

Let us examine the state apparatus which was created by the capitalists in order to keep the lower classes, the proletariat, under control. Marx had a few words to say on this subject in his book written in 1852, The Eighteenth Brumaire of Louie Bonaparte.

"This executive power, with its monstrous bureaucratic and military organization, with its artificial state machinery embracing a wide strata, with a host of officials numbering half a million, besides an army of another half million, this appalling parasitic growth, which enmeshes the body of French society like a net and chokes all its pores, sprang up in the days of the absolute monarchy, with the decay of the feudal system, which it helped to hasten...All the revolutions perfected this machine, instead of smashing it up. The parties that contended in turn for domination regarded the possession of this huge state edifice as the principle spoils of the victor."

Clearly, this "monstrous bureaucratic and military organization...this appalling parasitic growth." is not the state apparatus which can be used to crush the capitalists! Instead, the state apparatus which the capitalists have set up to crush us, the working class, has got to be smashed. After the revolution, a new and different state apparatus has to be established, one which is not bureaucratic, not military, not a parasitic growth, one which can and will be used by the vast majority, the working class, to crush the desperate and determined resistance of the capitalists, the insignificant minority.

Before the experience of the Paris Commune, Marx and Engels expressed themselves in rather general terms, as the "proletariat raised to the position of ruling class". After the Paris Commune, they stressed the Dictatorship of the Proletariat.

The Communist Manifesto refers to the Proletariat raised to the position of ruling class as merely the "first step", which is to say, other steps must follow. Perhaps the most important of those steps is to exercise Dictatorship over the bourgeoisie, to crush them completely, to absolutely preclude any effort on their part to return to power. There can be no doubt that they will make every effort to do just that.

It would be a great mistake to underestimate the resistance of the capitalists. After the revolution, classes will continue to exist, the resistance of the bourgeoisie will "increase tenfold" as they are determined to regain their "paradise lost".

They will plot and scheme endlessly to subvert the Dictatorship of the Proletariat, to return to power, to regain their wealth, to return to the "good old days" of exploiting the working class, to their lives of luxury and decadence. They have never worked a day in their lives, and after the revolution, when forced to perform manual labour, their resistance, their hatred, their bitterness will be boundless.

We say manual labor, because after the revolution we want everyone to be useful, and as many of them have no skills, aside from that of lying and deceiving, there is not a great deal else they are qualified to perform. So perhaps sweeping the streets is a job they can handle.

It is absolutely essential to keep them under the heel of the Proletariat, to prevent them from returning to power, hence the need for the state apparatus, the need to exercise Dictatorship over the bourgeoisie. This is the only way in which the Proletariat, the working class, can truly win the battle of democracy.

At the time the Manifesto was first written, it was not clear just what form the seizure of political power by the Proletariat would take. The experience of the revolutionary movement had not revealed this, so it was stated in rather general terms.

It was the experience of the Paris Commune that revealed the form of political power.

Although it did not achieve its goals and was brief, Marx saw that it was his task to analyze this experiment, to learn the lessons in this, the first socialist government, and to reexamine his theories in the new light this great revolutionary experience provided. That being the case, Marx subjected the experience of the Commune, meagre as it was, to the most careful analysis, in The Civil War in France.

As Marx phrased it, "The Commune was formed of the municipal councilors, chosen by universal suffrage in the various wards of the town, responsible and revocable at short notice. The majority of its members were naturally working men, or acknowledged representatives of the working class...Instead of continuing to be the agent of the Central Government, the police was at once stripped of its political attributes and turned into the responsible and at all times revocable agent of the Commune. So were the officials of all other branches of the administration. From the members of the Commune downwards, the public service had to be done at working men's wages. The vested interests and the representative allowances of the high dignitaries of state disappeared along with the high dignitaries themselves...

" Having once got rid of the standing army and the police, the physical force elements of the old government, the Commune was anxious to break the spiritual force of repression, the parson power...

" The judicial functionaries were to be divested of their sham independence...Like the rest of the public servants, magistrates and judges were to be elective, responsible and revocable."

For the first time in history, the working class, the Proletariat, seized political power, and the form of that political power was revealed. Now we know. The elected leaders were members of the working class, or acknowledged representatives of the working class,

the public service was performed at working man's wages, and each and every public servant, including judges and magistrates, could be immediately recalled. They were always accountable for their actions, and in the service of the people, not the rulers of the people.

The special repressive force for the suppression of the proletariat, the millions of toilers, by the handful of rich, the bourgeoisie, must be superseded by a special repressive force for the suppression of the bourgeoisie, the tiny minority, by the vast majority, the Proletariat, the Dictatorship of the Proletariat.

In modern day terms, we can just imagine approaching our democratically elected leaders, the members of Parliament, Congress, Senate, our Mayors and Governors, our Judges and Magistrates, our Ministers and Presidents, and suggesting to them that they should work for working mans wages and be responsible and subject to recall at any time. Not likely!

The goal of the Occupy Movement, or any other Revolutionary Movement, is to overthrow the capitalists, to seize state power, and smash the old state apparatus which is currently used to crush us, the working class. A new Dictatorship of the Proletariat, must be established. Only then can the major banks and corporations be seized, placed under the control of the working people.

CHAPTER 5
Lenin and the Russian Revolution

For the benefit of those who are just now becoming politically active, I will mention that in the early twentieth century, there were no less than three revolutions in Russia. As conditions in Russia most closely resemble our own, these particular revolutions are of great concern to us.

Capitalism developed in Russia somewhat later than in Britain and Western Europe, but by the late nineteenth century it was quite well established. As a result of this, in addition to the nobility, there was a rather powerful class of capitalists, bourgeoisie, and of course a very numerous and also powerful class of workers, proletarians. Still, most of the population, around three quarters, were peasants. Of course, as there were peasants, there were also landlords.

As previously mentioned, the interests of all working people, proletarians as well as peasants, are diametrically opposed to the interests of the capitalists. Yet in Russia, there was a complication, in the form of the Czar, or Emperor. His name was Nicholas the Second, although he was commonly referred to as Nicholas the Bloody. It was a title he earned, as his power was almost absolute. He used that power to crush anyone and everyone, even at the mere suspicion of opposition. This served to blur the antagonism between the workers and the capitalists.

As a result of this, the Russian people had almost no democratic rights. They were being crushed not only by the capitalists, but also by the Czar.

It was clear to the Marxists that it was first necessary to overthrow the Czar. A Russian democratic republic would be a step in the right direction, as a republic does not recognize any monarch, as the head of state. Of course the Czar would never agree to this.

Nicholas was accused of a great many things, but no one accused him of being a fool. He was supremely well aware that the Marxists, those who were at that time referred to as Social Democrats, were his greatest enemies. For that reason, he determined to imprison as many of them as possible. With his practically unlimited power, this was not terribly difficult. Most of them were either executed, or exiled. Lenin was exiled. As a consequence, the working people were deprived of their leaders.

If he thought this would stop the revolutionary movement, he was sadly mistaken. Such movements happen, with or without any leaders.

As a result of this revolutionary movement, on January 22, 1905, the people of Russia rose up, or as we say now, "took to the streets". It was a priest, Father Gapon, who led 150,000 peaceful protesters through the cold and snow covered streets of St. Petersburg, the capital of Russia, with a petition to Czar Nicholas. The wording of the petition clearly shows that they wanted and indeed expected the Czar to help them. It reads as follows:

"Oh sire, we working men and inhabitants of St Petersburg, our wives, our children and our parents, helpless and aged men and women, have come to you our ruler, in search of justice and protection. We are beggars, we are oppressed and overburdened with work, we are insulted, we are not looked upon as human beings but as slaves. The moment has come for us when death would be better than the prolongation of our intolerable sufferings.

"We are seeking here our last salvation. Do not refuse to help your people. Destroy the wall between yourself and your people."

Clearly, the citizens of Russia were appealing to the Czar as children appeal to their parents for help, as the citizens saw the Czar as a father figure. They could not possibly have been more mistaken.

The Czar responded with characteristic brutality.

As the crowd marched through St. Petersburg to the winter palace of the Czar, they were confronted by a large body of troops. These were the dreaded Cossacks, the personal body guard of the Czar. No doubt the Czar saw these peaceful protesters as a threat and ordered his Cossacks to attack. These Cossacks, mounted on horses and armed with sabres and rifles, did just that.

Within a short time, hundreds of innocent civilians were wounded or dead, slaughtered by the Cossacks. This day has gone down in Russian history as "Bloody Sunday".

As a result of this, the Russian people knew that the Czar was not at all interested in their grievances. They no longer looked upon him as a father figure but as an oppressor, a butcher, which is exactly what he was.

As the social scientists phrase it, he was now "fully exposed".

Perhaps the Czar thought that such a display of brute force would be enough to crush the revolution, that things would return to normal, that the capitalists could return to making money and he, the Czar and his immediate family, could return to their life of luxury.

If that is what he thought, he was sadly mistaken. Instead of dying down, it flared up and spread across Russia, but now with a more political character. Workers went on strike and peasants attacked the homes of their landlords. The transport system across the country practically came to a halt and protestors stormed the jails and the prisoners were released.

Peaceful protest had been transformed into full scale revolution. The people were demanding democratic rights such as freedom of speech, freedom of assembly, the freedom to strike, the right to form political parties and the right to a democratically elected Constituent Assembly. People of all walks of life took to the streets demanding change. These included workers, students, teachers, peasants, doctors, engineers, lawyers and revolutionaries.

The Czar responded by bringing in troops to break the strikes and crush the resistance of the workers and peasants, as well as anyone else who opposed him.

The Revolution raged for three years and the regime was shaken to its core but not toppled. After the revolutionary motion died down, reaction set in, as it always does.

The Czar and the capitalists thought that was the end of the Revolution, and as they saw it, things "returned to normal". The factories went back to producing, the railroads were running again, the strikes pretty well ended, and the capitalists continued to make money, which is about all they really consider important. This went on for several years, and they were very likely lulled into a false sense of security.

The Czar and the capitalists did not know it, but there had in fact been a profound change in the situation. The country only appeared to return to "normal", while in fact the working people, those who took part in the "Revolution of 1905", were now seasoned veterans. They no longer had any illusions. The Czar was no longer a father figure, and they saw him as the butcher that he was.

It helped that they were blessed with a great many Marxists, led by Lenin, who explained to them the principles of scientific socialism. These Marxists were in exile, for the most part, but managed to sneak in the printed word.

Of course there are differences between Russia of 1905 and North America of present day, but the attitude of the members of the public is similar. The people of Russia appealed to the Czar and expected him to listen to them, to respond to their legitimate grievances. Just so, the members of the public, here in North America, at the time of the Occupy Movement, appealed to their democratically elected leaders and expected them to respond, in a dignified, respectful manner.

Most members of the Occupy Movement had never protested before. By and large, they were honest, hardworking, law abiding citizens who vote in elections and expect their democratically elected leaders to represent them, in the various capitals. They come from all walks of life, young and old, of various ethnic backgrounds.

With a vague sense that something is wrong, these people took to the streets in a peaceful, respectful manner, as is their democratic right, and fully expected their leaders to respond in kind. They were merely trying to let the politicians know that something is not right, and the system is not working properly. It is just not right that the "super rich" have so much and the working people have so little. Or so they thought. From the government response, it became clear that the system is working just as it is supposed to work.

In Russia of 1905, the response of the Czar was supremely brutal. Yet the response of the government officials, here in North America, was not a great deal better. The police ordered the protesters to disperse, then they tore down their tents, and followed it up with tear gas, pepper spray, clubs, handcuffs and jail. The democratic rights of the people of North America, to assembly and peaceful protest, were trampled.

In both cases, the public has learned the bitter truth. The capitalists, the bourgeoisie, are running the country and will tolerate no challenge to their authority. They have shown their true colours and stand exposed.

Now it would appear that the Occupy Movement has died down. In fact, the people who first took to the streets were psychologically devastated, forced to face the fact that they have been lied to all their lives, that the government is in the service of the capitalists, the bourgeoisie, that any change will take place only when the whole rotten capitalist system is overthrown.

It is in this manner that people are tempered, and there is no harm in this. It is similar to the manner in which steel is forged, by first melting the metal down so that when it cools, the steel is much stronger. In much the same way, people are tempered in the struggle against the capitalist class.

The Occupy Movement was a revolutionary movement and now people are coming to realize that it is class warfare. The same people are returning to the streets, but now they are returning as seasoned veterans, ever more determined to enact change, with no illusions, knowing what to expect.

A similar situation happened in Russia. Following the Revolution of 1905, a period of reaction set in, as it always does, after an unsuccessful revolution. But then the revolutionary motion picked up again. It came to a climax in late February of 1917, with the overthrow of Czar Nicholas. The world was astounded! How was it that a monarchy, one which had maintained itself for three centuries, and further survived a three-year revolution, could have been toppled in a mere eight days?

At that time, Lenin was still in exile, living in Switzerland, but following the events in Russia, as best he could, with the limited information he had available. Even though he could not be there personally, he managed to give the revolution direction, through his letters, now known as "Letters From Afar".

Lenin explained that the "First Revolution", by which he meant the Revolution of 1905-1907, "deeply ploughed the soil, uprooted age old prejudices, awakened millions of workers and tens of millions of peasants to political life and political struggle, and revealed to each other -and the world- *all* classes (and all the principle parties) of Russian society in their true character....It exposed...(those) who are prepared to stoop to any brutality, to any crime, to ruin and strangle any number of citizens, in order to preserve the 'sacred right of property', for themselves *and their class!*" (italics by Lenin)

This is to say that the Revolution of 1905, provided the working people of Russia with valuable experience. Many millions of people, those whom had previously been apathetic, became politically active. The lies and hypocrisy of their rulers, and the class they served, became clear. These people no longer had any illusions. Those who took part in the 1905 Revolution, were transformed into seasoned veterans.

Lenin went on to say that the 1905 Revolution was something of a "dress rehearsal", for the "first stage" of the 1917 Revolution. The common people of Russia had gained valuable experience in the first Revolution. Due to that "training", the "first stage" of the Second Revolution proceeded supremely well.

Of course, he was referring to the overthrow of the Czar as being merely the first stage. Other "stages" were to follow.

Yet there were other factors at work. Not the least of these was the fact that the world was at war! Nicholas had decided to join forces with Britain and France, against Germany and her allies, in an effort to gain more colonies. Yet Russia had suffered several major defeats, so that there was a great deal of opposition to the war.

For that reason, both the British and French were afraid that Nicholas would arrange a separate peace with Germany. So they decided to take action. They decided to *depose* Nicholas. This gave rise to an extremely unusual situation, leading to the overthrow of Czar Nicholas.

As Lenin phrased it, "That the revolution succeeded so quickly and …so radically, is only due to the fact that …*absolutely dissimilar currents, absolutely heterogeneous* class interests, *absolutely contrary* political and social strivings have *merged*…the conspiracy of the Anglo - French imperialists… to seize power *for the purpose of continuing the imperialist war… slaughtering fresh millions* of Russian workers and peasants…. This on the one hand. On the other, there was a profound proletarian and mass popular movement of a revolutionary character for *bread,* for *peace,* for *real freedom.*" (italics by Lenin)

(We should explain that the word "imperialist" means monopoly capitalist)

This brings to mind an expression: Truth is stranger than fiction!

The truth is that the Anglo - French imperialists were determined to depose Czar Nicholas, just as the common people of Russia were equally determined to depose him!

The imperialists wanted Nicholas off the throne, so as to continue the war, while the common people wanted Nicholas off the throne, because they wanted *peace*!

This was not so much a union of different classes, towards a common goal, but a "merger" of the "political and social strivings" of different classes. To put this in popular terms, "politics makes for strange bed fellows!"

Yet the fact remains that the Anglo - French imperialists, working through their embassies in the capital of Saint Petersburg, organized a "palace coup". Various high ranking Russian officials and military personnel, were bribed. Nicholas was deposed. That was precisely the thing the imperialists wanted. Strangely enough, it was also the very thing the common people wanted!

With Czar Nicholas off the throne, a "democratic republic" was established. The people finally had the democratic rights which they had been demanding for so long. At least on paper, anyway.

The Russian Revolution of February, 1917, was a bourgeois revolution, a revolution which placed the capitalists in power. A democratic republic was established, much to the joy of the capitalists, as the democratic republic is the best possible political shell for capitalism, according to Lenin. If nothing else, the capitalists are better able to rule, if only through the direct corruption of officials.

As Lenin stated, "Once capitalism has gained control of this very best shell, it established its power so firmly, so securely, that no change either of persons, of institutions, or of political parties in the bourgeois democratic republic, can shake it."

The Russian people were no longer being crushed and exploited by the Czar and the capitalists, they were merely being crushed and exploited by the capitalists. It was a step in the right direction, but only a step. It was not a vast improvement.

The country was still at war with Germany and her allies, the people were cold and hungry, the troops were being led by the same incompetent officers, the Constituent Assembly was still being delayed, the landlords still owned the land, and the capitalists now had a free hand.

It is safe to say that this, the second Russian revolution of the twentieth century, was also spontaneous, leaderless, as almost all the surviving Marxists, including Lenin, had been banished.

This was fine by the capitalists, as they were in their glory. They were now in a perfect position to conduct business, to make money, to gear up the factories to full production, especially as the country was still at war with Germany, and any goods produced were sure to be destroyed in the war.

As a bonus, they no longer had to deal with the Czar. It was a capitalists dream come true.

As far as they were concerned, the Revolution had gone far enough. Now it was time to divert the Revolutionary Movement, away from socialism and the Dictatorship of the Proletariat, and onto something harmless, such as "defending the mother land". The last thing the capitalists want is for the workers, the proletarians, to be focused, to fulfill their revolutionary destiny, that of overthrowing the capitalists, the bourgeoisie, and establishing the Dictatorship of the Proletariat.

At that time Lenin was the leader of the Russian Marxists, referred to as Bolsheviks. He was closely following the progress of the second Russian revolution, and was well aware that the first step in the revolution, that of overthrowing the Czar, had been accomplished. The question uppermost on his mind was, could a Socialist Revolution in Russia be successful?

With that in mind, Lenin read everything Marx had written on the subject, that of the conditions necessary for the first Socialist Revolution to be successful.

Marx was sure that the capitalists in neighbouring countries would do everything in their power to crush a socialist state, as the Dictatorship of the Proletariat is their absolute worst nightmare, and they were afraid that it would spread to neighbouring countries.

With that in mind, Marx thought that the first successful Socialist Revolution would have to take place in several countries of the world at the same time. This would mean that the revolutionary motion could not be confined to one country, but to several countries in one particular part of the world. He very likely had in mind the German Revolution of 1848, which spread to several other countries.

Then again, Marx was of the opinion that if the country was big enough, then a Socialist Revolution had a reasonable chance of success. It was just possible that such a Socialist country could withstand the inevitable invasion of neighbouring countries.

Lenin had his answer. Russia was the country which was in revolt, and it was very large and quite highly industrialized.

True, the Revolution had not spread to neighbouring countries, but then the neighbouring countries were in a state of war with each other. He figured that at the moment, they were preoccupied with destroying each other, so that gave the first Socialist Revolution a reasonable chance of success.

It was time to carry the Revolution through to its historical conclusion, to a Socialist state, and establish the Dictatorship of the Proletariat.

Lenin was anxious to return to Russia to lead the revolution, but the problem was that he would first have to pass through German occupied territory. Yet Lenin was a citizen of Russia, a country which was at war with Germany. So how to return to Russia?

Diplomatic channels were opened and the German Kaiser was assured that the Russian officials, the so called Kerensky government, had no greater enemy than Lenin. For once, the advisers of the Kaiser were telling him the truth.

Accordingly, Lenin was placed on a sealed train and allowed to pass through German controlled territory, to Russia. On April 16, 1917, the train pulled into the station of Saint Petersburg. Lenin was home.

Of course, at that time, the country was officially ruled by the flunkies of the capitalists, referred to as the Kerensky Provisional Government. Although they were deeply divided upon a number of issues, all shared a passionate hatred for the Bolsheviks, as the Marxists of the day referred to themselves, and especially their leader, Lenin.

As that was the case, modern scholars are puzzled by the fact that the Kerensky regime did not immediately arrest Lenin, or even kill him on the spot, as soon as he stepped off the train. Without doubt, the thought did "cross their minds".

The "spirit was willing", so to speak. Yet there was a slight "complication".

That complication came in the form of a *"workers government, a Soviet of Workers Deputies"*. (Bear in mind that the word Soviet means Council, in English)

The Russian Revolution had given birth to a new creation, *Soviets of Workers!* These Soviets or Councils, were nothing other than a *separate workers government!*

As Lenin stated, "side by side with this government (that of Kerensky) ... there has arisen the chief, unofficial, as yet undeveloped and comparatively weak *workers government...Soviet of Workers Deputies...*an organization of workers, the embryo of a workers government". (italics by Lenin)

In Russia, early 1917, the Kerensky Provisional Government was not completely in control! Their power was being challenged by the newly created Soviets of Workers Deputies! For that reason, much as the agents of the Provisional Government wanted to arrest or even kill Lenin, they were unable to do it publicly. The Soviets were too strong!

Lenin immediately went to work, as the leader of the Bolsheviks. He determined that the members of the public, the workers and peasants, or "the masses", as he referred to them, were not fully prepared to take political power. Their level of awareness, or "class consciousness", had to first be raised.

As previously mentioned, the political situation in Russia, at that time, was quite complex.

The nobility, in the form of the Romanov's, were still a threat. There were considerable people, mainly among the class of landlords, who wanted to place another Romanov on the throne. They had in mind Michael Romanov, the brother of Nicholas. They thought he might be more "sweetly reasonable" than his brother, agreeable to continue the war with Germany. Or he could join his brother!

Then there were the peasants, and the majority of Russians were peasants. At that time, most of them were under the influence of the Socialist Revolutionaries, a political party that was devoid of principle, technically referred to as opportunist.

Then there were the Mensheviks, those whom had previously been members of the Social Democratic Party. Yet they had split with the true Marxists, the Bolsheviks. The Mensheviks claimed to be Marxists, while opposing Revolution and the Dictatorship of the Proletariat.

There were other political parties, such as the Constitutional Democrats, or Cadets, who were extremely Right Wing. They had the support of the landlords, and they too had a considerable following.

Under those conditions, Lenin determined that any attempt to overthrow the Provisional Government was doomed to failure. The workers and peasants were simply not sufficiently prepared.

For several months, Lenin openly gave speeches, and advised the members of the Bolsheviks to raise the level of awareness of the common people. This was supremely difficult, as so many people, especially the peasants, were illiterate.

Then in July of that year, the Provisional Government was able to order the arrest of Lenin. The task of raising the level of awareness of the common people, in preparation for Revolution and the Dictatorship of the Proletariat, became ever more difficult.

In response, the friends of Lenin, and in particular Stalin, were able to disguise Lenin, as a peasant, and sneak him out of the city, off to Finland.

While in Finland, Lenin prepared for the approaching uprising, the continuation of the Revolution of February. At that time, he wrote one of his greatest works, State and Revolution.

By the fall of that year, the level of awareness of the common people had been raised, so that they were prepared to seize power. None too soon! Kerensky figured that as the Revolution was based in Saint Petersburg, the best way to crush the rebellion was to *surrender the city to the Germans!*

The Revolution was carefully planned and executed. On November 7, new style calendar, or October 25, old style calendar, the Bolsheviks made their move. Telephone and telegraph exchanges in the two major cities of Saint Petersburg and Moscow were seized, as well as the railroad terminals, key bridges, and other important installations. The Winter Palace of the Czar was stormed, as the Provisional Government was hiding there. The Revolution was almost bloodless.

A new government was established, of the workers and poor peasants. The new flag expressed this, with symbols of hammer and sickle, to represent workers and peasants.

At first, it was referred to as Soviet Russia, or Council Russia, in English. The Dictatorship of the Proletariat! As other Socialist Soviet republics joined Russia, the name was changed to the Union of Soviet Socialist Republics, the Soviet Union.

There is a lesson to be learned from this. Under far more difficult circumstances, the Russian Revolution succeeded, in no small part because of the newly created Soviets, Councils.

The creation of Soviets, or Councils, is exceptionally significant, as it constitutes a new order of government. It is certainly true that these Councils first appeared in Russia, in 1905, as a result of the revolutionary motion. As they are nothing other than "the embryo of a workers government", that makes them a *threat to the existing capitalist government!*

Now they are also appearing in America. These Councils must be strengthened, encouraged, united, trained and armed, in preparation for the approaching revolution. As I have covered this in another article, there is no need to repeat it here.

Of course the capitalists are claiming that the collapse of the Soviet Union in 1989, is proof that Communism does not work, and that they in fact have nothing to fear. They would have us believe that the world is now "safe for capitalism". Of course, that is the very thing they want to believe. Most people believe that which they want to believe, and the bourgeoisie are no different.

It was Lenin who stressed the fact that the capitalists would make every effort to restore capitalism, to regain their "paradise lost", to return to their life of luxury and decadence, to once again exploit and oppress the working class. Lenin was not joking.

After the Dictatorship of the Proletariat was established, in the form of the Soviet Union, the capitalists were quick to notice that the political power was held by the Communist Party. Of course, they wasted no time in weaselling their way into the Party, pretending to be dedicated Communists. As they are first class liars, and constantly honing their lying skills, this was not terribly difficult.

Naturally, the Marxists within the Party were determined to root them out, and many of them were exposed and kicked out of the Party. Others were more cunning and escaped detection. As a result of this, after the death of Stalin, in 1956, Khrushchev was able to restore capitalism in the Soviet Union.

Marxists then refer to this period as the time of the "chauvinist Soviet Union", that which is socialist in name, but chauvinist in deeds, where chauvinist means false. This is another way of saying that the people in charge of those countries at that time were liars. As the capitalists are consummate liars, this is not too surprising.

A similar thing happened in the socialist country of China, after the death of Mao. The capitalists who had weaselled their way into the Communist Party of China staged a coup, seized power, and restored capitalism.

Such social chauvinists have certainly given Communism a bad name. Yet the term Communist was chosen, by Lenin, in honour of those workers of Paris, whom in 1871, established the Paris Commune. It was the first time that workers seized state power, and we should honour their memory, by referring to ourselves as Communists.

CHAPTER 6
Capitalism and Class Consciousness

Here in North America, it is customary to deny the existence of classes. The capitalists, the bourgeoisie, would have us believe that class distinctions are confined to the old world, meaning Europe, and that as the new world of North America was colonized, all classes were magically erased. Nothing could be farther from the truth!

Most of us can easily understand the class differences between a slave and a slave owner, and between a king, a lord, and a peasant. But then there are class distinctions here in the industrialized world which are not quite so obvious.

This begs the question: What is a class?

According to Karl Marx, membership in a class is determined by "ones relationship to the means of production".

That definition, which has the virtue of simplicity, may leave the astute reader wondering, just what the heck is the means of production?

As previously mentioned, it is a reference to the factories, mills, foundries, and mines which process the raw materials, such as minerals, ores and steel, into the finished products such as clothing and automobiles. When used in a broader sense, it may include the railroads, airlines, storage facilities, shipping lines, banks, trucking companies, and the internet. This is perhaps more accurate, as it is not enough to merely produce these items, they also have to be taken to market.

The people who own these means of production are called capitalists, and in fact are members of the capitalist class, also known as the bourgeoisie.

This brings us to another basic question: What is capital?

Most of us are familiar with the terms capital and capitalists, but may have only a vague notion of the subject. Under the current state of political unrest, this is absolutely not acceptable.

Remarkably enough, even though the terms capital and capitalist are widely used, it is difficult to get a proper definition of those words. No doubt, most of the common people, those who are just now becoming politically active, will consult with the internet. It is a fine source of information, so it makes perfect sense to use it.

One definition of capital is that of "already produced durable goods or any non financial asset that is used in the production of goods or services".

I confess that definition leaves me somewhat confused. I mention it only to reassure readers that if they find the current situation confusing, they are not alone. I am convinced that the system is meant to confuse people.

Another definition is: "Capital is wealth, whether in money or property, owned or employed in business by an individual, firm, company, corporation, bank or any other enterprise."

I find that definition a bit more comprehensible.

Still another definition of capital is "money used to buy something only in order to sell it again to realize a financial profit".

Now that is a definition I can understand, as it speaks to the key word, which is profit, which is the only thing which concern the capitalists.

Anyone who has even a passing acquaintance with any capitalist, well knows that they are completely focused on making a profit. It is the sole subject of any conversation! They call it their "bottom line", and consider it a great injustice that any business should be forced to pay taxes.

So much for the "popular" definition of the terms!

I mention this for the sake of drawing a comparison, between the bourgeois definition, and the proper scientific, which is to say Marxist, definition.

As Marx explained, in Wage-Labour and Capital, the bourgeois economists define capital in the following terms: "Capital consists of raw materials, instruments of labour, and means of subsistence of all kinds, which are employed in producing new raw materials, new instruments, and new means of subsistence. All these components of capital are created by labour, products of labour, accumulated labour. Accumulated labour serves as a means to new production in capital."

That is the only honest definition of capital. Even the bourgeois economists are forced to admit that capital is..."accumulated labour".

The more labour, the more capital! Less labour, less capital! It stands to reason: No labour, No capitol! Yet the capitalists are making every effort to eliminate labour! They swear by mechanization! If they succeed in eliminating labour, they will succeed in eliminating capital! Perhaps they have not thought this through? No Labour, No capital, No capitalists!

By an exceptionally strange but happy coincidence, it just so happens that the Communists are focused on the same goal. We too want to eliminate the capitalists!

It just so happens that we are more focused. We are going right to the source! We plan to overthrow the capitalists, seize political power, establish the Dictatorship of the Proletariat, and crush the capitalists!

Marx goes on to explain, in Wage-Labour and Capitol, that "The interests of capital and the interests of wage-labour are diametrically opposed to each other". This is to say that the higher the wages for the workers, the lower the profits for the capitalists.

We stress that it is wealth that is employed in business for the purpose of generating more wealth which constitutes capital, and not just wealth such as money in a bank which may form the life savings of a person. In much the same way, the house a person owns does not in itself constitute capital, as the person who owns that house is not using it to generate more wealth.

Then again, the bank may use that money, which may amount to the life savings of an individual, as a means of generating more wealth, not for the person who owns the money, but for the bank.

In a similar manner, the same bank may use the house which a worker owns in order to generate more wealth, not for the owner of the house, but for the bank.

As for those who object that this is not fair, we can only respond that fair has nothing to do with it. The act of using our money in order to create more wealth for the capitalists, the bourgeoisie, is perfectly legal, as the capitalists not only own the banks, they make the laws.

The point is that the person with a little money in the bank is not a capitalist, just as the person who owns a house is not a capitalist, as the person who owns that property is not using it to generate more wealth.

There can be no doubt that the capitalists, the bourgeoisie, have amassed a vast quantity of wealth. In fact, to put it in simple English, "they have more money than they can ever hope to spend"! It is not enough! Those who have millions want billions and those who have billions want more billions. It is safe to say that the more money they have, the less inclined they are to part with any of their hard stolen wealth.

By contrast we, the working people, the vast majority, are increasingly impoverished, destitute, scraping by on next to nothing, degraded, yet we share the little bit we have with our brothers and sisters who have even less.

No one has ever accused the capitalists of being stupid, and they are supremely well aware that the less they pay their workers, and the harder they force their workers to work, the higher their profit.

So on the one hand we have the capitalists who are crushing and exploiting their workers, and on the other hand we have the workers who are merely trying to earn a living. That which is good for one is absolutely not good for the other. We mentioned it before, and it bears repeating, that our interests are diametrically opposed.

As for those who suggest that our differences can be resolved, I can only suggest we examine the facts. The capitalists are very few but extremely wealthy. Their greed is boundless. Regardless of how much money they have, it is not enough. Their profits have got to be ever greater, and they are never satisfied with the money they have. Now they are stooping to the depths of stealing hundreds of billions of dollars of tax payer money.

No doubt we all watched in shocked disbelief as these corporate executives flew into our national capitals, in their private jets, begging for corporate welfare. All of these executives earn many millions, each and every year, and yet they were crying poverty. As insane as this sounds, stranger than fiction, the fact remains that the politicians bowed down to them, handing over to them the mountains of taxpayer money they were demanding

The capitalists, the bourgeoisie, are arguing that the biggest banks and corporations are Too Big To Fail [TBTF]. By implication, those countless members of the working class, the members of the public, who are losing their houses, jobs, vehicles and life savings, and in fact are going bankrupt, are Too Small To Succeed [TSTS].

If nothing else, we can thank the capitalists for drawing such a clear line between us and them. Further, the politicians, our democratically elected leaders, have made it clear that they are merely flunkies of the capitalists.

The battle lines have been drawn, and it is against this background that the Occupy Movement must be examined.

The Occupy Movement was nothing other than class warfare. A revolutionary movement and as previously mentioned, the people who were taking part in this Movement, were not conscious of their actions.

Throughout history, people have risen up against their rulers and frequently overthrown the class in power, the whole time unaware of the fact that they were making history.

The people who took part in the French Revolution of 1789 were not aware that they were performing the impossible.

At no point did any of them wake up one morning and decide to overthrow the monarchy. Yet overthrow the monarchy they did, as millions of people rose up spontaneously. It is difficult to think of this as anything except that which it is, an Act of God.

In much the same manner, the people of Russia rose up and finally overthrew the Czar, in early 1917. It was only in November of that year, when Lenin and the other Marxists provided them with the awareness of themselves as a class, which is called class consciousness, that the working people were able to overthrow the capitalists, the bourgeoisie, and establish a socialist state, the Dictatorship of the Proletariat.

All subsequent Revolutions have followed the same pattern, as the capitalists are well aware.

This creates a little problem in that the history of all countries shows that the working class, strictly by its own efforts, is able to develop only the most basic consciousness, such as the necessity of combining in unions, fighting against the multinationals, encouraging the government to pass more fair laws, etc.

This is commonly referred to as "trade union consciousness", which is not terribly accurate but it is a term which is well entrenched in scientific literature. Besides, it is more comprehensible than a more accurate term, such as "embryonic consciousness", so I will stick with trade union consciousness. This is precisely the state of all current revolutionary movements, and that is completely unacceptable.

The working class, the proletariat, has got to become aware of itself as a class, which is to say, it must develop "class consciousness".

This class consciousness must be brought to the working class from an outside source, from those who are aware of the existence of classes, as well as of the revolutionary theories of Marx and Lenin. Yet there is a complication.

That "complication" comes in the form of those who claim to be Marxists, while in fact revising the theories of Marx, either openly or not so openly. They serve the capitalists, the bourgeoisie, and in return for this act of self-degradation, belly crawling and boot licking, can expect a reward of absolutely nothing. The capitalists merely accept this as that which they deserve.

It was Lenin who condemned these "revisionists" most strongly in his book, What Is To Be Done? As he phrased it, they "corrupted socialist consciousness" by "declaring the idea of the social revolution and the Dictatorship of the Proletariat to be absurd, by restricting the labor movement and the class struggle to narrow trade unionism". Our current crop of Marxist revisionists is little different, aside from the fact that they generally remain silent on these critical points, that of Revolution and the Dictatorship of the Proletariat.

Yet the working class continues to spontaneously gravitate towards socialism. It is up to intellectuals, conscious people, Marxists, referred to as Communists, to give direction to these spontaneous movements. We have got to raise the level of awareness of the people taking part in those spontaneous movements.

A fine example of the working class spontaneously gravitating toward socialism is provided by the federal election, in Canada, in 2011.

Canada is not a republic, but a Constitutional Monarchy. This is to say that Her Majesty, the Queen of England, is recognized as the Head of State. She is represented in the country by the Governor General. The Prime Minister is the Head of Government.

There are three branches of the government, executive, legislative and judicial.

The executive branch, also known as "the government", is composed of the Governor General, the Prime Minister, and the Cabinet. Their duty is to "deliver programs and services to the population, within the framework of laws, expenditures and tax measures, approved by legislature."

The legislature is composed of the "Crown", represented by the Governor General, the House of Commons, and the Senate. They have the power to "make laws, raise taxes, and authorize government spending". The House of Commons is considered to be "dominant". The role of the Governor General is mainly ceremonial, while the Senate "rarely opposes the will of the House of Commons".

In the interest of being complete, I should mention that the judicial is a reference to the courts.

The Senate is composed of 105 members, while the House of Commons has 308 members. Each member of the House of Commons is referred to as a Member of Parliament - MP - and each is directly elected by Canadian voters. The members of the Senate are appointed by the Prime Minister.

Any bills passed by the House of Commons must be approved by the Senate, and in order to be a member of the Senate, such an individual must own a certain amount of property. The Senate has been referred to as a House of "sober second thought".

Assuming that is the case, then the House of Commons must be considered to be populated by a bunch of drunks who lack impulse control!

In fact, our democratically elected leaders may have their shortcomings, but by and large, they are not a pack of falling down drunks!

The Senate is nothing other than a bureaucratic establishment, a political plum, a reward to which people may aspire, in return for being faithful to the Party.

No doubt most people are familiar with the term "bureaucrat", without quite knowing the meaning of the word. It is just a reference to a non-elected government official, someone who is not accountable to the voters and generally, in modern society, creates mountains of paperwork in an attempt to justify their jobs. In short, a bureaucrat is a parasite, someone who contributes nothing to society, but lives off the labour of others.

As this book is being written, there are no less than three members of the Senate who have been suspended from the Senate, and are facing possible criminal charges, and numerous others who are under investigation.

The wits among the working class refer to them as the Three Dummies Who Got Caught.

In Canada, we also have several political Parties, which includes the Conservative Party, which claims to represent the business people, the party of the "Right Wing". We also have a Party which formerly claimed to be "Socialist", the Party of the "little guy", to represent the "Left", the New Democratic Party, or NDP. Then there is a Centrist party, the Liberal Party, to represent the "Middle Class", We also have a French party, the Parti Quebecois, to represent the people of Quebec in their struggle for independence. For everyone else, we have a fifth Party, the Green Party, which seems to represent everything else or nothing else, no one is quite sure which.

The Conservative Party and the Liberal Party are considered to be the two "giant" Parties, and over the last many years, power has passed back and forth between them.

The other three Parties are commonly referred to as "also rans".

The Party which holds the majority of seats in Parliament is allowed to form the government, which means holding 155 seats or more in the House of Commons. The leader of that party then becomes the Prime Minister.

The party which comes in second, in terms of the number of seats in parliament, becomes the Official Opposition.

If no one Party has a majority, then the Party with the most seats in Parliament forms a government, called a Minority government. Then the other Parties hold the balance of power.

Over the last good many years, the power has passed back and forth between the Conservatives and the Liberals. These Parties are generally referred to as tweedle dee and tweedle dum. This is another way of saying that there is not much to choose between them.

Then in the last federal election, which started out as the usual bore, things changed, dramatically and quickly. There were the usual campaign speeches, ads on television and debates by the leaders. No doubt some people watched this, but no one of whom I am aware.

The Liberal Party was out of power at that time, so they brought in their "big hitter", a man who was out of the country at that time, apparently teaching at a top Ivy League University in the States.

The campaign lasted six weeks, and started in the usual manner, commonly called a "snooze fest". Very few Canadians were paying attention. But then something happened which changed all that. Three weeks into the campaign, the press reported that all across the country, people were making some strange sound. That strange sound was Socialism!

This caught our immediate, undivided attention.

Almost immediately, the opinion polls swung into action, and sure enough, all of the polls reported that Socialism was indeed on the minds of Canadians!

At that point, no one was more surprised than the politicians. It came as quite a shock that voters, especially working people, were gravitating away from the Liberal Party, as well as away from the Party of the French, the Parti Quebecois, and moving towards the self-proclaimed Socialist Party, the NDP. Further, among the politicians, no one was more surprised by this than the NDP! They were accustomed to coming in a distant third, at best.

In the fourth week of the six-week election, the polling results showed the Liberal Party, as well as the Parti Quebecois, steadily losing ground to the   NDP!

The leader of the Liberal Party, as the man of action that he is, "took the bull by the horns" and came up with a plan to turn the election around. He changed his footwear! He announced that for the remainder of the election, he would wear runners with the colours of the Liberal Party! He also stated that the election had just begun!

It is rather sad to think that a candidate for the highest office in the country, a man who stood a reasonable chance of becoming Prime Minister, a man who is qualified to teach at a most prestigious university, is not capable of counting, at least not all the way up to six!

As for his idea that countless people would change their mind and cast their vote for his Liberal Party, that he could turn the election around with a change of footwear.... I have to question his sanity! The idea that Canadian voters decide to cast their ballots, based upon the footwear of the candidates, rather than their stand on the issues, is nothing

---

short of absurd. I would even go so far as to say that it is an insult to voters!

On the day of the election, we were all anxious to determine the election results, and as the polls first closed on the east coast, we were hoping to get a sneak peek.

It is to the credit of the democratic process, here in Canada, that there was a news blackout, at least until the last polls closed on the west coast. The posting of any early election results from the east coast could have influenced the voting on the west coast, so the press was muzzled.

The results were just as the polls had predicted, and it was official and stunning. The Liberal Party had pretty well changed places with the New Democratic Party, and the Parti Quebecois was all but wiped out. Even the leaders of these two Parties had lost their seats in Parliament. Even a change in footwear had not turned the election around!

In each case, it was a total embarrassment.

This did not stop the leaders of the Parties who had lost so much, including their seats in Parliament, from complaining. They pointed out that in certain cases, the candidates who were running for the NDP, had not even campaigned. Members of the press quite cheerfully pointed out that one candidate was not even in the country, at the time of the election! She had been on vacation and was finally located in Las Vegas, where she was informed that she was now a Member of Parliament.

By law, candidates for political office do not have to campaign. They merely need to have the signature of one hundred registered voters, and that is precisely what many of them had. Such candidates are commonly referred to as "paper candidates".

Even in Quebec, which is a French nation, contained within the borders of Canada, there is no legal requirement that candidates for Parliament be required to campaign, or even to speak French.

Most of the people who ran for Parliament, as members of the NDP, very likely did so mainly out of a democratic sense. They probably thought it was their democratic duty to offer voters an alternative. They were assured that they had no chance of success, so there was really no point in campaigning. Likely most of them believed this.

By a remarkable coincidence, the world wide revolutionary movement touched the Canadian working people, the members of the public, the common people, as we refer to ourselves, during the middle of a federal election. As a result, the people spontaneously gravitated towards Socialism, and in fact voted for the NDP, which, at that time, claimed to be Socialist.

This is just one example of the spontaneous development of a revolutionary motion, as people spontaneously gravitate towards socialism.

I say a Party which claimed to be Socialist, as they are not now a Socialist party, and they never were. They are not a Revolutionary Party, and at no point have they ever mentioned the necessity of Revolution, or the Dictatorship of the Proletariat. They are careful to stay within the bounds of that which is acceptable to the bourgeoisie. As mentioned previously, class struggle is acceptable to the bourgeoisie. The Revolution and subsequent transition to the Dictatorship of the Proletariat is absolutely not acceptable.

After the election, the NDP, which had succeeded beyond its wildest dreams, and in fact became the party of the Official Opposition, decided to change their strategy, and drop the name Socialist.

This was honest of the NDP as a whole, but the reason they quit claiming to be a Socialist Party, was not out of a sense of honesty, but for a more practical reason. They wanted to become the Party in charge! With that in mind, they figured, in the simplicity of their souls, to "broaden their base", and appeal to the middle class, the same middle class which is practically wiped out!

This is the age of imperialism, of monopoly capitalism, and as a result of this, the middle class has been devastated. This simplifies the class struggle, in that there is a clear distinction between "us" and "them". The vast majority, the working people, are pitted against the tiny minority, the billionaires, the monopoly capitalist, the bourgeoisie.

So the word Socialist was dropped, and the NDP "moved to the Centre", as it is called, in an attempt to replace the Liberal Party, the "Party of the Centre". They even considered joining the Liberal Party! They refused to face the fact that the only reason they are so successful, the only reason so many people voted for them, is because the revolutionary motion has touched down on the shores of Canada. People are embracing Socialism, spontaneously moving towards Socialism, and against capitalism.

The point is that the idea of the party of the Left, the NDP, to move to the Centre, and embrace the middle class, which for all practical purposes does not exist, makes absolutely no sense. So of course, that is exactly what they did.

Incidentally, in the next federal election, the NDP was soundly defeated, so that they returned to their previous role as "also rans".

If nothing else, this helps to draw a clear line between those who claim to be Socialists, the Utopian Socialists, and the Scientific Socialists, those of us who are Marxists.

The bourgeois political leaders here in Canada are no different from the bourgeois political leaders of any other country, which is to say that they are not overly bright.

All joking aside- and that previous comment was meant as a bit of a joke- and in the interests of accuracy, they all have one thing in common. They all serve the capitalists, the bourgeoisie. As such, they have the bourgeois ideology, so that they are not capable of conceiving of anything outside of the best interests of the capitalists. They absolutely cannot face the fact that the Revolutionary Movement has touched down on the shores of Canada.

The Right Wing, Conservative Party, was not terribly effected by this. They stayed in power, as the people who vote Right Wing are not about to switch their vote to Socialist.

This helps to drive home the point that the capitalists are well aware of themselves as a class while we, the working class are not class conscious. This gives them an advantage. That is completely unacceptable. The members of the working class must be made aware of themselves, as a class.

The spontaneous movement towards Socialism is gaining strength. The province of Alberta, which traditionally has been a bastion of Conservatism, recently had a Provincial Election. The results were shocking, as the revolutionary movement has touched down in that province also. The business oriented, Conservative Party was voted out, and the NDP was voted in. This is just one more example of the Revolutionary Movement gaining power in the country, spontaneously gravitating toward Socialism. Now the leaders of the other Parties around the country are worried that they may lose power to the NDP. That is about the least of their worries, but they are not aware of this.

In fact, the leaders of the various Parties should be concerned about the working class, becoming aware of themselves as a class and of the necessity of Revolution and the subsequent Dictatorship of the Proletariat.

This calls for a little explanation.

The fact is that Scientific Socialism and the class struggle of the working class, arise separately and not together. It is the duty of the Marxists, the Scientific Socialists, to bring about their merger.

As for those who think that we are overstating the case, let us examine precisely what Engels said, in 1874, in his introduction to his book "The Peasant War in Germany"...

"keep in mind that socialism, having become a Science, must be pursued as a Science, it must be studied. The task will be to spread with increased enthusiasm, among the masses of the workers, the ever clearer insight thus acquired, to knit together ever more firmly the organization both of the Party and of the trade unions..."

It should be noted that by the Party, he meant the Party of Scientific Socialism, the Communist Party.

Engels placed the study of Scientific Socialism on the same level as that of the political struggle, which is a matter of fighting for our democratic rights, and also on the same level as the economic struggle, that of fighting for decent wages, working and living conditions. These are the three great struggles of the Occupy Movement.

Capitalism must be replaced by Socialism, yet without a Revolutionary theory there can be no Revolutionary Movement! Without a clear goal of scientific socialism, in the form of the Dictatorship of the Proletariat, the Occupy Movement is merely "spinning its wheels".

Perhaps an example will help to drive that point home.

While it is true that in Russia in February of 1917, the Czar was overthrown and citizens did achieve some democratic rights, they remained crushed by the capitalists. It was necessary for the Marxists, led by Lenin, to bring to the working class the awareness of themselves as a class, and to carry the Revolution through to its logical conclusion, to a Socialist state, with the working class in charge. The form is the Dictatorship of the Proletariat, with all factories, mills, mines and banks, as well as all other businesses of any considerable size, established as state property, run by the working class.

It was only after the Russian working class became aware of itself, as a class, with its own class interests, that the revolution could be carried through, to a socialist state. For that reason, on October 24, old style calendar, or November 7, new style calendar, 1917, the Russian proletariat was able to overthrow the capitalists. The Russian capitalists were then crushed under the Dictatorship of the Proletariat.

It may help to think of any revolutionary motion as a boxing match, but in this boxing match, one of the boxers is blindfolded. No doubt at some point the boxer who is blindfolded is bound to land a crushing blow, but that is strictly a matter of good luck and not good planning.

We can think of the Proletariat, the working class, as the boxer who is blindfolded, and the capitalists, as the boxer who can see very well.

This may seem as an overly simple, childish comparison, and maybe it is. But then again, maybe not. The capitalists are supremely well aware of themselves as a class, and they are also well aware of the Marxist revolutionary theory of the Dictatorship of the Proletariat.

By contrast, the members of the working class, those taking part in the Occupy Movement- or any other Revolutionary Movement! - are not aware of themselves as a class. Nor are they aware of the revolutionary theories of Marx and Lenin. Very few of them have even heard of the Dictatorship of the Proletariat! They are lashing out in all directions! They are even striking out at their friends!

This Revolutionary Motion has also been compared to a ship on the sea. All such ships require a navigator, someone to give direction. Otherwise, the ship is bound to drift aimlessly, according to the winds and currents.

Perhaps it would help to think of the followers of Marx, Communists, as the "navigators", those who provide the direction. The "Compass" they use is the revolutionary theories of Marx and Lenin.

The working class movement, the Occupy Movement, which is currently a spontaneous movement, must be brought to the level of conscious awareness.

Until that awareness is reached, the Occupy Movement, or any other revolutionary movement, will continue to resemble a boxer who is throwing punches in the dark, or a ship drifting aimlessly on the sea.

We can only stress that these revolutionary theories, of Marx and Lenin, grew out of the philosophic, historical and economic theories that were elaborated by the educated representatives of the propertied classes, the intellectuals. According to their social status, the founders of modern Scientific Socialism, Marx and Engels, themselves belonged to the bourgeois intelligentsia.

The task of the Marxists is to make the Proletariat, the working class, aware of itself as a class, conscious of its position, conscious of its destiny, that of overthrowing the capitalists, that insignificant minority of parasites which is crushing the vast majority, and replacing it with the Dictatorship of the Proletariat.

No doubt there are certain simple, misguided souls who think that the pure and simple Occupy Movement can work out an independent ideology for itself, that the working class should take control of their own destiny.

In the interests of explaining these Scientific terms - for the benefit of those who are too shy to ask- we will add that ideology is a system of ideas and ideals, especially one that forms the basis of economic or political theory and policy.

The fact is that in a society torn by class antagonisms, there can never be a non-class or above class ideology. There is no middle course, so the choice remains, either Scientific Socialism, Marxism, for the working class, or the capitalist, bourgeois ideology. To belittle Scientific Socialism in any way, to deviate from it in the slightest degree, is to strengthen the capitalist, bourgeois ideology.

We do not dispute the fact that the current Occupy Movement is spontaneously gravitating towards socialism. That is not enough. The bourgeois, capitalist ideology is constantly asserting itself, and it is far older, more fully developed, deeply entrenched and has far more opportunities to force itself upon us. Under these conditions, the conditions of spontaneous development, the Occupy Movement will only become subordinated to bourgeois, capitalist ideology.

We may think of class consciousness as similar to removing the blindfold from the boxer, allowing him to see, better able to land a solid blow. Or perhaps we can think of it as placing a navigator on board the ship.

But as the working class cannot provide that light to itself, cannot remove the blindfold, cannot form the class consciousness, it follows that the light, the class consciousness, must come from an outside source, from outside the working class. That begs the question, just who is it, or perhaps more accurately, just which class can provide the light, the direction, the class consciousness, the Scientific Socialism to the working class?

The Communist Manifesto provides the answer:

"As capitalism develops, entire sections of the ruling class are, by the advance of industry, precipitated into the proletariat, or at least threatened in their conditions of existence. These also supply the proletariat with fresh elements of enlightenment and progress...In times when the class struggle nears the decisive hour, the process of dissolution going on within the ruling class, in fact within the whole range of old society, assumes such a violent, glaring character, that a small section of the ruling class cuts itself adrift and joins the revolutionary class, the class that holds the future in its hands."Just as, therefore, at an earlier period, a section of the nobility went over to the bourgeoisie, so now a portion of the bourgeoisie goes over to the proletariat, and in particular, a portion of the bourgeois ideologists, who have raised themselves to the level of comprehending theoretically the historical movement as a whole."

So the answer to the question of which class can provide the light, the class consciousness, this act of removing the blindfold from the boxer, the proper direction, can come only from the bourgeois intelligentsia, from the middle class, or at least from people who have been well educated, from intellectuals and professional people who are progressive, those who are prepared to educate the working class and prepare them for their destiny.

We also have intellectuals among the working class, and this includes professional people such as teachers, doctors, engineers, students and lawyers, as well as writers such as myself. It is up to such people, who are aware of class distinctions, to carry this message to the rest of the working class, the proletarians.

It is a mistake to think of the bourgeoisie, as a class which is growing, expanding, becoming ever more numerous. It is not. They are only growing in terms of their wealth, which is beyond the comprehension of most people. In turn, their wealth is growing only because of their greed, which is equally beyond comprehension. It is absolutely boundless.

The capitalists are not content to exploit the working class, and steal the mountains of tax payer money. They also steal from each other. For this purpose, they have training courses, called seminars, or "retreats", and at these seminars, professional thieves teach them the finer points of fraud.

The capitalists are taught how to lie most persuasively, and they practice these lies in front of each other, as well as in front of a mirror. The importance of being able to appear sincere is stressed. As the thieves phrase it, "once you can fake sincerity, you have it made".

The thieves will also organize games, on these seminars, whereby each participant is assigned an imaginary amount of money, in much the same way that people play monopoly. The object of the game is to separate the other players from their money, just as in the game of monopoly. The difference is that in this game, the players are encouraged to meet in private, form alliances, and enter into business deals, with the purpose of separating the other players from their wealth.

Of course, the most successful players are those who are not only able to present themselves as sincere, but also as honest, rather simple souls who are people of their word, reliable and trustworthy. Then at a suitable time, when the stakes are high enough, such a "simple soul" can betray their partner, or as they call it, "stab them in the back".

Those who are the most devious, cunning, and deceitful, most successful at stabbing their partners in the back, are highly praised and honoured. The other members of the seminar look upon them as role models.

These skills of fraud and deception, which are honed in seminars, are used upon each other, with the result that some capitalists are ruined. They have no choice but to seek honest employment, to join the ranks of the working class, even though reluctantly and generally with a great deal of bitterness. It matters not, as long as they bring the awareness of the class struggle with them, of the necessity of Revolution and the subsequent Dictatorship of the Proletariat.

Of course, there are other capitalists who have simply gone broke, for whatever reason. It matters not. As long as they join us, and fight alongside of us, they are our friends, our Brothers and Sisters, our Comrades, and we must welcome them as such. This is class warfare, and in this war, we can use all the friends we can get!

No doubt, there are members of the working class who are prejudiced against intellectuals. They respect only manual labor. To such people I have a word of advice, or more accurately, three words: Get over it! Whether you know it or not, and very likely you do not know it, you are serving the capitalists. They, the capitalists, are members of your fan club. They most emphatically agree that the intellectuals, the Marxist, should not interfere, give direction to the Revolutionary Occupy Movement. They are quite sure that they can divert the Movement onto some harmless course, harmless to themselves(!), as long as the intellectuals, the Marxists, do not give it any direction. It is in their best interests to keep the working class in the dark, blindfolded, thrashing around aimlessly. The last thing the capitalists want is for the working class, to be focused, to have clear cut goals, to be conscious of themselves as a class, to be determined to overthrow the capitalists, and crush them, through the Dictatorship of the Proletariat.

Only the Marxists, the Scientific Socialists, the intellectuals, are capable of removing the blindfold, providing the proper direction, allowing the members of the Occupy Movement, the working people, to fulfill their destiny of overthrowing the capitalists and establishing a new society, based on the Dictatorship of the Proletariat.

As previously mentioned, this awareness can only come from outside the working class.

At present, here in North America, it may help to think of the intellectuals, the Marxists, as the equivalent of the Party, as it was the intellectuals to whom Engels was referring.

Chapter 2 of the Communist Manifesto spells it out quite clearly.

"The Communists do not form a separate party opposed to the other working class parties.

"They have no interests separate and apart from those of the proletariat as a whole.

"They do not set up any sectarian principles of their own, by which to shape and mould the proletarian movement.

"The Communists are distinguished from the other working class parties by this only:

In the national struggles of the proletarians of the different countries, they point out and bring to the front the common interests of the common proletariat, independently of all nationality.

"2.In the various stages of development which the struggle of the working class against the bourgeoisie has to pass through, they always and everywhere represent the interests of the movement as a whole.

"The Communists therefore, are on the one hand practically the most advanced and resolute section of the working class parties of every country, that section which pushes forward all others; on the other hand, theoretically, they have over the great mass of the proletariat the advantage of clearly understanding the line of march, the conditions, and the ultimate general results of the proletarian movement.

"The immediate aim of the Communists is the same as that of all other proletarian parties: formation of the proletariat into a class, overthrow of the bourgeois supremacy, conquest of political power by the proletariat."

This spells out quite clearly the role of the Marxist. This makes it easy to identify the true Marxist, as opposed to the intellectuals who attempt to divert the working class movement, including the Occupy Movement, onto some harmless course, a course which is acceptable to the capitalists.

Here in North America, the situation is sharp and clear, as the capitalists have almost entirely wiped out the peasants, family farmers, and very nearly wiped out the middle class.

As long as we bear in mind that our relationship to the means of production is basic, then it is easy to determine our class and to distinguish our friends from our enemies.

Those of us who work for a living are our friends, while those who own the means of production, the capitalists, are our enemies.

It is a rather common misconception, among the working class, to think that those who are reasonably well paid are "middle class". Such is not the case. Those who work by the hour are working class.

In fact, the term middle class, or petty bourgeois, where petty means minor, refers to a class which owns or rents small means of production which it operates largely without employing labor, although we would add that often they are assisted by members of their family.

As a result of this, the middle class or petty bourgeois is torn in two. He is both a worker and a capitalist. As a worker, this poor soul has interests in common with the working people, the proletariat, while as the owner of a business, a means of production, however small, he has interests in common with the capitalists, the bourgeoisie. In fact, he dreams constantly of becoming rich and successful, of becoming bourgeois, of joining them. This is not about to happen!

Yet the fact remains that he is truly "caught between a rock and a hard place". It is not too surprising that he tends to vacillate, one day supporting the revolutionary forces, the next day supporting the capitalists.

There is one other strata which concerns us, and that is "intellectuals and salaried personnel", of the capitalists. Lenin states that they "correspond to the petty bourgeois". As such, they tend to be well educated, highly skilled administrators. This does not stop the capitalists from firing them, for any reason, or for no reason. When that happens, we must welcome them into our midst, as our Comrades!

They bring with them the awareness of classes. As well, after the revolution, their administrative skills will prove to be most valuable.

This brings us to the peasantry, a class which is all but wiped out in North America but a force to be reckoned with in most countries of the world. As this Movement is international in scope, it is important for us to understand that which is happening, so that we can better support our comrades in arms in other countries.

The peasantry can be divided into three groups, rich, middle and poor.

The rich peasants, sometimes referred to as kulaks, or "tight fists", also known as "rural bourgeoisie", hire farmhands and day labourers, and live by the labour of others. They try to squeeze as much work out of their farmhands as they can, while paying them as little as possible. Frequently these farmhands are poor peasants.

The middle peasants, or "rural petty bourgeois", are those who own or rent land but do not employ labor. His position is most unstable as only in good years and only under most favourable circumstances is his crop sufficient to make ends meet. Not too many years are good years, so this poor fellow generally has to resort to working away from home for several months of the year.

This bring us to the poor peasant, one who works part of the year on his farm, and part of the year works for wages. He has to work for wages, as his farm does not supply him with enough to survive. He is no longer an "independent farmer", but a "rural semi proletarian".

We should add that the word "rural" means country, while the word "urban" means city.

There are also people who are referred to as "rural proletarians". For the most part, they consist of former peasants who have lost their farms, and scrape by working for rich peasants.

Also, there still exist in certain countries of the world a class of landlords, a class which owns the land and derives its income from ground rent on that land. They are not peasants but small time rural capitalists.

The fact is that peasants are nothing other than small time capitalists. It is characteristic of peasants that they want to own the land they are tilling, as well as the land next to them, the land of their neighbours. This does not make the poor and middle peasants the enemy. On the contrary, they are the natural and desirable allies of the proletariat. We have got to live in peace with them.

It is the rich peasants, the kulaks and landlords, who are our enemies.

The working class, the Proletarians, have got to lead the Revolution. The other classes will follow, especially as the Revolution gains strength. In underdeveloped countries, we can also expect Revolutionary Motion, similar to the Chinese Revolution of 1949, which has incorrectly been referred to as a peasant revolution.

True, at that time in China, the peasants composed the vast majority of the population, and the Proletariat was numerically very small, but it was the working class, the Proletariat, which led the revolution to victory.

We can expect the petty bourgeois to vacillate, between fighting for the Revolution and fighting against it.

In short, we can expect the lower strata of the peasants to join the revolution, as well as the lower strata of the middle class, although we can also expect them to vacillate. We know this from the experience of previous Revolutions. The only class which is consistently Revolutionary is the working class, the Proletariat.

This brings us to the semi proletarians, those who work at occasional part time jobs, frequently addicted to alcohol and drugs. They tend also to be small time thieves, in and out of jail, and the capitalists find them quite useful, in terms of attempting to crush the Revolutionary Movement.

The Communist Manifesto also mentions these people, and lets us know what to expect:

"The lumpen proletariat, the social scum, that passively rotting mass thrown off by the lowest layers of the old society, may here and there be swept into the movement by a proletarian revolution; its conditions of life however, prepare it far more for the part of a bribed tool of reactionary intrigue."

Some of these people rather enjoy "cracking skulls", as they call it, and we can expect the capitalists to hire them to clobber peaceful protesters, and we must be prepared for them. As soon as cracking skulls is no longer fun, which is to say that as soon as people begin to defend themselves, then such people can be expected to join the Revolutionary Movement. When that happens, it is up to us to welcome them, as our Brothers and Sisters, our Comrades.

We must be aware that certain of our enemies of today may well be our friends of tomorrow. This happened in the French Revolution of 1789, the Russian Revolution of 1917, and has happened in every successive Revolution.

It is absolutely imperative that we stress upon the working class that the capitalists are members of a different class and further, that our interests are diametrically opposed. It is in the interests of the capitalists to work us as hard as possible while paying us as little as possible. This will ensure them the highest possible profit, which is the only thing that concerns them.

We repeat, as was proven beyond any shadow of a doubt by the experience of the French Revolution, it is the common people who make history. We, the members of the working class, are now rising up against the class which exploits and oppresses us, the capitalists. The Movement has spread around the world, and is one of the finest, strongest Movements the world has ever seen.

All of the finest military commanders are well aware that it is vitally important to know as much as possible concerning the enemy. I call this information, while the military refers to this as "intelligence". Whatever it is called, we have got to know our enemy, just as we have got to know ourselves. With that in mind, let us examine the bourgeoisie.

That capitalist class knows very well that classes exist, and is quite content to propagate the lie that classes do not exist in North America. They are well aware that knowledge is power, and are determined to keep us in the dark.

The capitalists think that "ignorance is bliss". At least, our ignorance is bliss, as far as they are concerned. The less we know about our situation, the better they like it.

The capitalists, the bourgeoisie, look upon us with the utmost contempt, just as the nobility regards all commoners with equal contempt. This supreme arrogance may arise as a natural result of being rich and powerful and never doing an honest days work in their life. It follows that the bourgeoisie refer to the working class, as "bottom feeders", "trailer court trash", the "rank and file", the "masses", "rag tag and bob tail", "gutter sweepings", "dregs of humanity", the "great unwashed mob", among other things. Yet we are the people who earn them all their money and in fact, we are the people who make history.

Among the working class, it is a common mistake to regard the capitalists as individuals who are basically fine fellows, just a bit misguided. They are not at all misguided. They are entirely focused, determined to separate as much money as they can from us, to work us as hard as possible, to pay us as little as possible. In short, they are the enemy, and we must show them just as much mercy as they show us, which is to say, none whatsoever.

We must focus on our goals, which are spelled out quite clearly in the Communist Manifesto:

"The distinguishing feature of Communism is not the abolition of property generally, but the abolition of bourgeois property. But modern bourgeois private property is the final and most complete expression of the system of producing and appropriating products, that is based on class antagonisms, on the exploitation of the many by the few.

"In this sense, the theory of the Communists may be summed up in the single sentence: Abolition of private property....

"You are horrified at our intending to do away with private property. But in your existing society private property is already done away with for nine tenths of the population; its existence for the few is solely due to its non-existence in the hands of those nine tenths...

"In one word, you reproach us for intending to do away with your property. Precisely so; that is just what we intend...."

Just as in the French revolution, feudal property, the property of the landlords and nobility was sacrificed for the benefit of the bourgeoisie, so too in this Socialist Revolution, the property of the capitalists, the bourgeoisie, will be sacrificed for the benefit of the proletariat, the workers.

It has been objected that upon the abolition of private property, all work will cease, and universal laziness will overtake us.

According to this, bourgeois society ought long ago to have gone to the dogs through sheer idleness, as so many members have never done an honest days work in their lives!

About the closest they ever come to work is counting their money and complaining about paying taxes. If whining is considered work, then they are in fact very hard working souls!

CHAPTER 7
Occupy Movement

The fact is that the "common people", as we call ourselves, are working class people, and the technical name for that is proletarians. We work for wages, and sell ourselves by the hour. The social scientists refer to us as "wage slaves", as indeed we are, and in fact we take great pride in our work. We are patriotic citizens of our countries, and are only asking for that which is rightfully ours. We are also poor, for the very fine reason that we are not thieves. Those who steal are not poor.

It is not too surprising that in North America, the countries of the United States and Canada, are deeply in debt. The working people have been bled dry, there is just not much more they can squeeze from us, while the capitalists, the bourgeoisie, do not pay taxes, or at best very little.

Our politicians justify this by saying that these people, the billionaires, who earn so much more than working people, are in a "better position to invest their money", their capital, and create jobs. As if the capitalists are interested in creating jobs!

In fact, the capitalists are interested in one thing and one thing only, and that is profit, money, their "bottom line"! Most of their money is placed in offshore banks, out of the reach of the tax collectors, while the money which they declare is in a very low tax bracket. The politicians, whom they control, are careful to pass laws which make such theft legal.

Now we have a situation that is similar to that of ancient Greece at the time of Solon, in that the vast majority of people are impoverished and the ruling class is supremely wealthy. As the social scientists phrase it, the "contradictions are sharp and clear". This is a revolutionary situation.

The fact that this Revolutionary Motion is happening, did not come as any great shock to those or us who are Scientific Socialists. We expected it.

We can trace this movement back to January of 2011, when the people of Tunisia revolted and overthrew the dictator. This inspired an additional wave of protests throughout the Middle East and North Africa. The dictators of Egypt and Libya were deposed, but of course this was not the end of the class conflict. Even though the dictators were overthrown, the capitalists are still in charge. The people of those countries now have some democratic rights and with the dictators out of the way, the class conflict is now sharp and clear.

Although it is not clear, it is entirely possible that this Revolution was similar to the French Revolution of 1789, when the bourgeoisie joined the peasants and the proletarians in an alliance referred to as the third estate, in the revolt against the nobility.

From the standpoint of the North American Revolution, it is not relevant, as we have almost no peasantry and no nobility.

Then again, from the Middle Eastern standpoint, it is supremely relevant.

Assuming such an alliance took place, it is no longer in place, as the dictators have been overthrown, and the capitalists are now the enemy, the new dictators.

Now it is similar to the situation in Russia in the spring of 1917, when a spontaneous revolution overthrew the Czar and the people enjoyed a measure of freedom in the form of democratic rights, at least on paper.

It is very likely that the capitalists in the countries of Tunisia, Libya, and Egypt welcomed the Revolution, and a few of them may even have taken part in this. The omnipotence of wealth is more secure in a democratic republic.

On the other hand, the democratic republic is also the battleground on which the final battle of the working class against the capitalist class will be fought.

The workers of those countries are now veterans, seasoned soldiers. They have no illusions, and know what to expect. Now when the workers take to the streets in protest, they are better prepared. They are wearing helmets, and carrying clubs and shields. In earlier protests, the government sent out men on horseback and on camels, armed with clubs and whips, to crush the Rebellion.

The fact of the matter is that they have achieved some democratic rights, which is of the utmost importance, but they are finding that their living conditions are basically unchanged. It is clear that the capitalists are still in charge.

The countries of Libya and Tunisia are rather small, at least in terms of population, and not very highly developed in the industrial sense, so it is doubtful that a socialist revolution could succeed in either country, by itself, for the very fine reason that other capitalist countries would invade the country and attempt to overthrow the socialist government. The bourgeois attempt to justify this by saying that "Communism must be contained"!

By contrast, the country of Egypt is rather large, in terms of geography as well as population, and quite highly industrialized. This means that there is a very large working class population, the proletariat.

No doubt there are other classes of people who work hard there, such as peasants and middle class people, the petty bourgeois, and without doubt many, but by no means all, are supporting the working class people in the Revolution.

It is clear that Egypt is a key country in the region, which is not to downplay the efforts of the working people in other countries. A Socialist Revolution in that country has a far better chance of success, mainly because of the size of the country, especially if the Socialist Revolution spreads to other countries in the region. We can expect Socialist countries to support one another.

Revolutions happen on a regular basis. Every so often, people get into motion, frequently by the millions, and challenge the ruling class. It is difficult to see this for anything but that which it is, an Act of God.

Under the present circumstances, the surprise was that it started in the rather small, underdeveloped country of Tunisia, and spread so quickly to so many other parts of the world.

In the past, Revolutions have been confined to one country, or at best, several countries in one part of the world. This Revolution has spread around the world, and very quickly.

Without doubt, conditions have changed, and the Revolutionary Motion has changed with them.

So exactly what conditions have changed?

The capitalists have tied together the economies of the world, especially with their spread of capital to all countries of the world, with their control of various stock markets and their ownership of the national debts, as very few countries of the world are not deeply in debt.

As a result of this, most countries of the world are on the verge of bankruptcy.

Certainly in North America, the countries of the United States and Canada, are practically broke, as are various countries in Europe. It would appear that by tying together the economies of the world, the capitalists have also tied together the Revolutionary Movements of the world. Now the Revolution has spread from the Middle East, North Africa, to Europe, Asia, North and South America. In other words, all around the world.

The Occupy Movement is a spontaneous uprising and it is spontaneously gravitating toward Socialism. It requires direction, and it is up to the Marxists, the intelligentsia, to provide that direction, to bring the theory of Scientific Socialism to the working class, to the people who have taken to the streets, to the people who are demanding change. The goal of the Occupy Movement must be Revolution, the smashing of the state machine, seizure of all capitalist property and establishing the Dictatorship of the Proletariat. Anything less is completely acceptable to the capitalists.

It is significant that the Occupy Movement quickly spread to America. The American working class rose to the occasion, and wasted no time in placing themselves in the forefront of the international movement.

Now the Movement has morphed into other protest movements, still with the Americans in the forefront. Protesters in other countries are watching closely. All the more reason to set the example! Yet bear in mind the words of Lenin: *"the role of vanguard can be fulfilled only by a Party that is guided by an advanced theory!"* (italics by Lenin) I mention this as a means of stressing the importance of a proper revolutionary theory! The Revolutionary Movement must have clear goals, that of Council -Soviet- Power and the Dictatorship of the Proletariat. The level of awareness of the working class must be raised. They must become "class conscious". The "blindfold" must be removed! They must become focused on landing a "solid blow" on their enemies, the monopoly capitalists, the billionaires, the bourgeoisie.

The capitalists must be challenged wherever they are. We must allow them no peace. We must challenge them at their resorts, which is the place they go to relax and entertain themselves, while consuming the finest alcohol, finest cocaine, and enjoying the finest prostitutes. They can afford nothing but the finest because they pay for it with the money they have stolen from us. This is also the place they go to gamble and plan their next robberies.

They must be challenged in their entertainment centres. Writers and actors must demand that movies, plays and tv series be produced with the working people in mind, not with the idea of glorifying the violence, exploitation and degradation of women.

We must also challenge them in the schools and universities. Students and teachers must be encouraged to demand that courses be taught which are relevant and honest, history be taught as it really happened, and not as the capitalists would have us believe it happened.

The fact is that we have been robbed of our history. Any reference to our true Revolutionary past is carefully ignored or glossed over. The history books are filled with distortions and outright lies.

We will know that we are getting our message across, when the banners and posters, carried by the protester, read:

Dictatorship of the Proletariat!

Scientific Socialism!

Soviet Power!

Workers of the World, Unite!

CHAPTER 8
Robbed of Our History

In particular, the American people have a proud history of Revolution. It is a testament to the efficiency of American propaganda that most American citizens are almost completely unaware of their Revolutionary history. In fact, American propaganda is a masterpiece of deception and outright lies.

Almost all Americans are aware of the Revolutionary War of 1776-1783, but what is glossed over is the fact that the war was in fact, truly Revolutionary.

In contrast to the French Revolution, the American Revolution was not entirely spontaneous. There were leaders, members of the colonial aristocracy who put aside their differences long enough to compose a Revolutionary document, to declare independence from Britain, referred to, quite reasonably, as the American Declaration of Independence. It is probably not desirable or necessary to reproduce the entire document here, especially as it is written in the flowery language of the time, complete with appeals to the Creator.

One of the key passages states:

"We hold these truths to be self-evident, that all men are created equal, that they are endowed by their Creator with certain inalienable rights, that among these are life, liberty and the pursuit of happiness. That to secure these rights, Governments are instituted among men, deriving their just powers from the consent of the governed. That whenever any form of government becomes destructive of these ends, it is the right of the people to alter or abolish it, and to institute new government, laying its foundation on such principles and organizing its powers in such form as to them shall seem most likely to effect their safety and happiness."

No doubt this is something the ruling class, the bourgeoisie, do not want the working people, to focus on, the fact that the governments derive their "just powers from the consent of the governed. That whenever any form of government becomes destructive of these ends it is the right of the people to alter or abolish it, and to institute new government..."

To think that the founding fathers of the United States stated quite clearly that the people, and by that they mean the citizens of the country, have the right to *abolish* any government which does not represent the people!

Without doubt, the Declaration of Independence is a truly Revolutionary document, one of which the American people can truly be proud.

This was written in the year 1776, and the people who wrote and signed this document were members of the colonial aristocracy. They were a mixed lot, and included merchants, land owners and slave owners. The fact that they united long enough to compose and sign this Revolutionary document is remarkable in itself, as most of them could not stand each other.

This speaks to the power of Revolution, in that people with deep differences, those who ordinarily do not speak to each other, unite against a common enemy.

Of course, the British government, called the Crown, considered this an act of High Treason, and was determined to hang each and every one of them, regardless of whether they were merchants, landlords or slave owners. The Crown was sure that the noose would fit one and all!

If nothing else, this provided the leaders of the Revolution with the motivation to stick together. As one of the leaders is reported to have phrased it, "we can hang together, or we can hang separately."

These early American Revolutionaries also were supremely hypocritical, as their reference to all men being created equal was their way of saying that they, the colonial aristocracy, were the equal of the nobility.

They certainly did not mean to imply that the slaves which they owned, or their indentured servants, or even the people who worked for them, were their equal. It was just their way of saying that the government, or in this case the king, could rule only with the consent of the governed, by whom they meant themselves. They also made it clear that the king did not have that consent, and therefore they were declaring independence.

The men who signed this Revolutionary document are called the Founding Fathers of the United States, and even though hypocrites, they were truly Revolutionary. That which they wrote many years ago is just as true today as it was when it was first written. The American people have the right to alter or *abolish* any government which does not represent them!

This is absolutely not something which the capitalists, the billionaires, want Americans to dwell upon!

Of course, the British Crown took a rather dim view of this "act of treason", as they saw it, and were well experienced in crushing revolts. They knew that the most effective way of quelling any discontent, was a simple matter of hanging the leaders.

The British did in fact make a determined effort to round up those individuals who signed that document, the leaders of the colonial rebellion, so as to hang them and crush the rebellion. The fact that they were unsuccessful speaks to the power of the Revolution, which was deep and broad, as well as the vast distances involved in sending troops from Britain to the United States. As well, the Colonials took advantage of the friction between Britain and France, and used that to their advantage.

The war raged for several years, and for some time it was touch and go, but eventually the Revolutionary forces prevailed, a peace treaty was signed and the United States of America truly came into existence, and not just on paper.

Most citizens of the United States refer to themselves as Americans, and refer to their country as America. These terms are not entirely accurate, yet out of respect for our American comrades, I too will use those names.

At the time of the Revolution, many of the leaders were members of the rising class of capitalists. They saw the great potential of a country with vast natural resources. They were also well aware that the British capitalists were determined that the colonies should provide the natural resources for the British mills and factories. Nothing more!

For that reason, it was necessary to break away from Great Britain.

Yet the "Colonial Capitalists" were well aware that they were not strong enough to do this, on their own. So they formed an alliance with the class of people they hated. The slave owners.

In addition, the industrial revolution, which gave rise to the ideas of liberty, equality and fraternity in Europe, also gave rise to those same ideas in the American colonies. It was not only the rising class of capitalists in the colonies, who were influenced by these ideas, but also the working people, the tradesmen, farmers, indentured servants, trappers, bankers and fishermen, among others. It was a vast assortment of people from various walks of life who had a common interest, and united for a time with the capitalists, in order to overthrow the rule of the British monarchy.

Some people compare this to the French Revolution of 1789, and say this American revolution, was merely a fore runner of the Big One, the Main Event.

In the American colonies, there truly was a union of the so called "third estate". Yet after the successful conclusion of that Revolution, the working people and the capitalists, returned to being enemies, whether they knew it or not. As well, the capitalists and the slave owners no longer had any reason to unite.

Of course, not everyone supported the colonial rebellion. There were those who remained loyal to the Crown, and most of these patriots, called "Tories", tended to be somewhat better off than most people.

We can compare this situation to that of today, in that we can expect certain members of the middle class, to not support the Revolution.

The Tories of yesteryear were the modern day equivalent of the counter revolutionaries of today, commonly referred to as "contras". One of the most glaring absurdities of the Reagan administration is to declare that the contras of today are the "moral equivalent of the American Revolutionaries of the Seventeen Seventies". Precisely the opposite is the case, but then, the lapdogs of the bourgeoisie tend to be not terribly concerned with honesty. In fact, the closest they ever came to honest, is in learning how to spell the word!

During the first American Revolution, many such Tories paid for their loyalty to the Crown by being coated with tar and feathers, and then being paraded through the streets. Many of them also lost most, if not all, of their property.

The lesson here is that in a Revolution, the normal rules of civilized, polite society do not apply. It is entirely possible that such acts of disrespect may happen again, subjecting the capitalists and their lapdogs to considerable humiliation. It could not happen to a more deserving bunch of people!

For the most part these Tories fled north, to Canada, which at that time was a loyal British colony, not touched by the Revolution.

The British were especially anxious to capture and hang the traitors who had previously been officers in the British army, those who had taken an oath to serve and protect the Empire and then "turned their coats", discarding the red of the Empire for the blue of the rebels, taking up arms against the very country which they had sworn to protect. As far as the British were concerned, this was the ultimate act of High Treason.

These turncoats included Benedict Arnold and George Washington. The former goes down in history as a first class traitor, and the latter is renowned as a great patriot.

Benedict Arnold is considered a traitor by the Americans because he turned his coat for a second time, once again donning the red of the British Army. By contrast, George Washington merely turned his coat once.

Those of us who are somewhat logical find this double
standard a little strange, but then it is the victors who write
the history books.

It is reported that Washington was shocked and furious
to find that Arnold had turned his coat for a second time,
rejoining the British. He really should have expected this, as
those who are traitors, are not to be trusted.

As a Canadian, I am related to a great many Americans,
and in fact we are very close. The family ties are very strong. So
in an effort to determine just how successful the bourgeoisie
has been in rewriting American history, I prepared a small,
informal quiz for my relatives. The results were interesting,
and while I do not suggest that it represents the view of the
majority of American citizens, I do suggest that it gives an
idea of the lack of awareness of their own history.

I was not too surprised to find that my relatives did
not know the story behind their national anthem, The Star
Spangled Banner. Most of them thought it was written in
1861, and the fort referred to was Fort Sumpter; that this
was the same year the country first broke apart, in that the
southern states seceded from the union; that the country
went to war because the states do not have the right to
secede from the union; that slavery was abolished in 1863,
the year President Lincoln issued his famous Emancipation
Proclamation; that the presidential palace was always called
the White House; some of them were not even aware that the
United States and Canada had ever been at war, and those
who were aware of this could think of no battles that had
been fought between the two countries, aside from the Battle
of New Orleans, and only because it became the subject of a
popular folk song.

In all fairness, I must add that at that time, in 1812, Canada was a colony of Great Britain, and technically, the United States was at war with Great Britain, although Canada was the "bone of contention", the location of most of the battles.

So in the interests of bringing clarity to the situation and hopefully irritating the bourgeoisie, and not with the idea of antagonizing our American comrades, I will state that they are completely mistaken. Each and every one of these lies and misconceptions will be addressed in turn.

Shortly after the American Revolution, the Revolutionary Americans became side tracked by the completely ridiculous idea of "Manifest Destiny". Many of them became convinced that Almighty God had chosen America to accomplish great things, and that it was the right, if not the duty, to expand from sea to sea, to spread their influence over the continent.

The origin of this bit of idiocy, that of Manifest Destiny, is not clear, but it is very likely that Thomas Jefferson was involved. He was the third president of the United States, and is, to this day, widely admired and respected.

Without doubt, Jefferson was a brilliant man, a true genius. He was one of the Founding Fathers, the principle author of the Declaration of Independence. He designed the large mansion of Monticello, considered to be an architectural masterpiece. As well, he was a scholar, scientist, fluent in several languages, and interested in science, inventions, religion and philosophy. He also owned hundreds of slaves, even though he publicly opposed slavery in his speeches and writings. He lived a life of luxury, eating the finest food, drinking the finest imported wines, riding the finest thoroughbred horses.

As a result of this, he was generally deep in debt and usually managed to avoid bankruptcy by selling some of his stock, which is to say, his slaves. On one day alone, he placed fifty slaves, human beings, on the auction block and sold each and every one of these people to the highest bidder.

It is true that under his leadership in 1778, a law was passed banning the importation of slaves into the state of Virginia. There are those who use this as an example of the humanitarian tendencies of Jefferson, of his commitment to end slavery. These same people carefully ignore the fact that he merely reduced the competition, so that the value of his stock, which is to say his slaves, increased dramatically, which is precisely the dream of every capitalist!

Upon his death in 1826, he was so deeply in debt that all of his remaining slaves were sold at auction.

No one can deny the fact that Jefferson was a brilliant man, a genius. It is also a fact that he lived a life of great luxury, off the backs of his slaves, and whenever he needed cash for his extravagant life style, he merely sold some of his slaves.

Jefferson could also see the "writing on the wall", and knew that it was simply a matter of time before the slaves would win their freedom, although not from a successful slave rebellion. World events were moving towards the abolition of slavery, like it or not.

As a genius and as an American, not to mention a racist, Jefferson was of course concerned with this state of affairs. He was well aware that several million slaves, "Negroes" as they were then referred to, would soon be free, and he did not want them "polluting" his country, his America, the country he helped create, the country he loved. He wanted to keep his country pure white, Caucasian. His solution to the "Negro" problem was quite simple: Send them to Africa.

Not only was Thomas Jefferson a genius, but he was also a psychopath and a racist.

His sanity is at best questionable, as he was clearly instrumental in formulating the doctrine of Manifest Destiny. Or it could be that he was just not a terribly logical person. Not all brilliant people are entirely logical.

To this day, historians continue to argue over the sanity of Jefferson, but there can be no doubt that the American leaders, including Thomas Jefferson and James Madison, decided to expand the borders of the United States.

In 1803, they purchased the Louisiana territory from France, and the geographical territory of the country doubled. It was not enough. They also decided to annex Canada.

In 1812, the young country of the United States went to war with Britain.

In both the United States and Canada, the British American War of 1812 is commonly referred to as the Forgotten War. The leaders of both of our countries would prefer that we, the citizens, the common people, not be aware of it. There are fine reasons for this.

As most residents of Canada, at that time, considered themselves to be British, there could be no talk of Canadians. There were a great many people who were referred to as French Canadians, those whom, at that time, did not consider themselves British, but French, or Quebecois, Quebecers.

It was the opinion of Thomas Jefferson, that the capture of Canada was simply a matter of marching. As he is reported to have stated, "The Canadians will welcome us as liberators." The British and French colonials, whom he referred to as Canadians, had other ideas.

As well, not every American was enthused with this war of expansion. A disaster was very narrowly averted. In fact, Jefferson and Madison grossly underestimated the opposition to that war. It was quite a shock when the northern states of Maine, New Hampshire, Vermont, Massachusetts, Connecticut and Rhode Island, generally referred to as the New England states, separated from the Union.

We stress the fact that in the year 1812, the United States first broke apart. New England was allowed to separate from the Union. The United States did not go to war with the breakaway republic of New England. The states were allowed to separate.

In legal terms, this is known as a precedent, and a precedent is that which sets a standard for future events.

Great Britain went to war with the United States, but not with New England, as New England was not part of the Union.

From a very early age, the American citizens are bombarded with American propaganda. Every school child stands up every school morning, faces the American flag, places their right hand over their heart and recites the pledge of allegiance.

It is as follows:

"I pledge allegiance to the flag of the United States of America, and to the republic for which it stands, one nation, under God, indivisible, with liberty and justice for all."

During the course of a lifetime, the average American citizen recites this pledge countless times. This in no way changes the fact that it is simply not true. The United States of America is completely divisible. The precedent has been set, the country broke apart before and will no doubt break apart again. The states have every right to separate from the union.

In 1812, the British fleet sailed across the Atlantic and set up a blockade along the coast of the United States, but not New England. It is true that the British later in the war did blockade the coast of New England, but only because the Americans were using the ports of New England to supply their country. The war with Britain did not proceed precisely the way in which Madison and Jefferson had planned.

General Sir Isaac Brock was a British general in charge of the troops in the British colony of Canada, and was faced with a huge task of fighting the Americans with a very small force of British regular army troops, supplemented with a force of irregulars, which included Anglos, or English speaking troops, all of whom considered themselves British, and French speaking troops, Quebecers, all of whom considered themselves French.

To complicate matters, Britain and France were at war, and Canada was merely a backwater of the Empire, and a very cold one at that. No doubt General Brock would have much preferred to be in Europe, at the centre of the action, rather than protecting an "iceburg of a colony". But "orders were orders", and he was determined to carry out those orders, which he did, in magnificent style.

The General was well aware that most of his "Anglo" troops, the Tories, had fled from the colonial rebellion of several years before and were now facing their old friends and neighbours, and even their relatives, who were determined to invade Canada. He was not at all sure that these troops could be trusted.

Still less did he trust the French speaking troops, as
Britain and France were at war. He seriously doubted that the
Quebecois would fight under the British flag, the Union Jack.

And then there were the First Nations people, those
whom were at that time referred to as Indians. They were
caught in the middle, used by both the British and Americans.

In the interests of showing respect for the soldiers of all
countries and for the time in which they lived, I will use the
names which they used at that time.

With that in mind, let us face the fact that for two and
one half years, the Americans, British, French and Indians
were killing each other. To say that this was terrible, is an
understatement. We have so much in common and that
includes a common enemy. Of course, the common enemy
to whom I am referring is the bourgeoisie, the ruling class
of capitalists.

In particular, General Brock immediately threw a monkey
wrench into the American plans by marching south and
capturing Fort Mackinac, followed by Detroit. This was not
at all that which Madison and Jefferson had in mind when
they declared war on Britain.

Most of Michigan fell into the hands of the British, and
President Madison wanted to court martial General Hull for
surrendering Fort Mackinac, without even firing a shot. But
who would court martial the president of the United States?
More on that later.

Although that was certainly an American humiliation, in
all fairness to the Americans, Oliver Perry led an American
fleet in the battle of Lake Erie, which resulted in a great
American victory, in that a whole British fleet surrendered
to the Americans.

The point is that the military on both sides, American and British, scored major victories when properly led, while faced humiliating defeats, when led by incompetent officers.

General Brock was killed in action in 1812 at the battle of Queenston Heights. Everyone agreed that on that day, a great general died.

On the day of his funeral, the British cannon fired off a 21 gun salute. The Americans were aware that his funeral was taking place, and after the British cannon fired off their salute, the American cannon also fired off a 21 gun salute.

In those days, soldiers of different countries had respect for each other. It must have been nice.

Even though Americans and Canadians have a great deal in common, which include a common language, it is also true that we have certain differences. Canadians tend to be a bit more critical and as a result of this, we have very few heroes. We can almost always find fault, but even we cannot find fault with General Brock.

Possibly the only "homegrown hero", one with whom even Canadians cannot find fault, is Laura Secord. She lived close to the Canadian - American border and very likely was fluent in English and French. Her husband had been wounded in the battle of Queenston Heights, and she was tending to him and her young children.

But then the Americans invaded, took over her cabin and forced her to cook for them. She in turn may have pretended to be unable to speak English. That is not clear, but what is clear, is that she overheard the American officers talking about their plans for the coming battle. After everyone else was asleep, she slipped out of the cabin and ran all night, a run which reportedly took twelve hours. This was extremely dangerous, as only trails existed in the wilderness, and she was trying to avoid American sentries. In the morning, she reached the camp of the Iroquois. The Iroquois took her to the camp of the British commander, and she told him of that which she had overheard.

It is clear that Laura Secord risked her life in that famous midnight run, at a time when her death would have caused great hardship for her husband and children. She placed her duty to her country above that of her life and her family. Even Canadians cannot find fault with that, although it is not clear that the information she provided to the British officers was of any great value. Historians suspect the British already knew the plans of the Americans, but this in no way detracts from her brave actions.

There is almost no chance that she did this for money, as at that time no one was rewarded in such a matter. She was no exception, and in fact for the next fifty years her sacrifice was pretty well forgotten. She worked hard and grew old in poverty. Then, in her old age, she was rewarded by the British crown with one hundred pounds. Even in those days, one hundred pounds or roughly one hundred fifty dollars, was not a princely sum.

Now she is recognized as one of the few home grown Canadian heroes.

It was in August of 1814 that events most decidedly "took a turn for the worse", from the American standpoint, after the British concluded the war in Europe with the French. A British fleet, carrying a sizeable detachment of British regular army troops, was sent to America, and in fact sailed up Chesapeake Bay. The troops set ashore and marched up Constitution Avenue. This is significant, if only because this Avenue leads directly to the Presidential Palace, in Washington.

It was James Madison, President of the United States, who had declared war, and the British were giving him precisely that. Of course, this was not at all what Madison had in mind. His response to the approaching enemy army leaves no doubt as to that subject. Madison immediately jumped on the nearest horse and ran from battle as fast as he could, as the coward that he was.

In fact, the Commander in Chief of the American armed forces ran from battle so fast, he left his wife behind!

Of course, the modern day historians try to gloss over this act of cowardice by claiming that he "relocated to another area so that he could better control the battle"!

No doubt these historians are trying to rewrite history, in a manner which the capitalists find acceptable. In return for this bit of belly crawling and bootlicking, they probably expect the capitalists to throw them a bone, possibly in the form of a government posting. This rarely happens, as the capitalists merely accept such abasement as their due.

It is significant that the wife of the president, commonly referred to as the First Lady, saved the Declaration of Independence, a truly historical, Revolutionary Document. Her name was Dolly Madison, and she deserves recognition for her act of heroism.

Of course, the modern historians continue to distort the truth by referring to the Declaration of Independence as a "Portrait of George Washington". The capitalists do not want the American public, the working people, to pay any attention to that Revolutionary Document!

After Dolly Madison saved the Declaration of Independence, she and the other wives of the American official cowards, all of whom had run, also ran for their lives.

Not that the British made war on women and children, but in a war zone, civilians can and do get injured.

This is one of the little details which the ruling class, the capitalists, do not want the citizens of the country to be made aware. It is not the only detail.

The British then proceeded to burn the Presidential Palace, as it was then called, as well as other government buildings. It was only after the end of the war, that the Presidential Palace was rebuilt, and was coated with white wash. Ever since then, it has been referred to as the White House.

The British fleet, still looking for a battle, sailed south, to Baltimore, and laid siege to Fort McHenry. They blasted the fort all night, and the onlookers were afraid the Fort would surrender. It did not surrender, and one of the onlookers was so proud, he wrote a poem.

His name was Francis Scott Keys.

The poem was titled "The Battle of Fort McHenry", and the title has since been changed to "The Star Spangled Banner". It has since been set to music, and is now the American National Anthem.

The British fleet then sailed south to New Orleans and disaster, at the Battle of New Orleans.

The hero of this battle was another American future president of the United States, Andrew Jackson. He is commonly referred to as Old Hickory. That battle was fought in January of 1815, after the peace treaty had been signed in Europe on December 24, 1814, so that technically, the war was over. As communication was very slow in those days, the American and British officers were not aware of this and the war carried on.

As a result, there was a great slaughter, mainly of British troops.

It is significant that there were a number of First Nation people who were of vital assistance to General Jackson, in the Battle of New Orleans.

Later on that same year, 1815, the breakaway New England Republic learned that the war was over and the borders would remain the same. As a result of this, the New England Republic agreed to rejoin the union, at the Hartford Convention of 1815. They had fully planned to join Canada.

Several years after the war, General Jackson was elected President of the United States. As a slave owner and an "Indian fighter", he was a racist to the very core of his being. He and his buddies noticed that the "Five Civilized Tribes", as they were called, which included the Cherokee, Chickasaw, Choctaw, Creek and Seminole, owned some valuable property. Those people had previously been advised to assimilate, and they had done just that. In fact they cleared land, built houses and barns, grew crops and bred livestock. They were well established as farmers, solid, law abiding, tax paying citizens, loyal Americans, one and all.

President Jackson was not at all impressed by this, any more than he was impressed by the fact that their assistance was instrumental in the American victory at New Orleans. As far as President Jackson was concerned, they were merely "savages", and the property they owned was too good for them.

One of his first acts as president was to pass a law, the Indian Removal Act of 1830. This gave the federal government the authority to kick the Five Civilized Tribes, American citizens, out of their homes and steal their property.

The trouble was that the Five Civilized Tribes did not cooperate. To the utter fury of President Jackson, they challenged this law in court. Worse, the Supreme Court of the United States ruled that this law, the Indian Removal Act, was unconstitutional, and therefore, President Jackson could not remove those people and steal their property.

President Jackson was not at all impressed. He is reported to have mentioned that the Constitution of the United States is merely a "scrap of paper"! Whether he said this or not, his actions reflected that attitude.

President Jackson issued the order for the removal of the Five Civilized Tribes and the confiscation of their property. Over a period of several years, American troops broke down the doors of American citizens, dragged those Americans out of their homes, stole their property and marched those Americans west, to "Indian Territory", today known as Oklahoma. Those who resisted were shot, and those who ran were hunted down and whenever possible, either captured or killed.

That "relocation", so called, is referred to as the "March of Tears", as so many Americans died on that trail. The very young and the very old were the first to die, as well as pregnant women. Countless other people died as well, all of whom were American citizens, killed by American soldiers. In fact, the area from the east coast to Oklahoma is littered with the remains of American citizens.

There is one more little detail, which the American capitalists attempt to hide.

This order was carried out by General Winfield Scott, one of the heroes of the War of 1812. This same general is given credit for transforming the American army into a fine professional outfit. He has been referred to as the Grand

Old Man of the Army, and historians rate General Scott as the best American commander of his time. He even ran for president, on one occasion, and to this day is honoured in that country.

President Jackson and General Scott were both guilty of mass murder, and crimes against humanity. The people they murdered were civilians, American citizens.

No doubt many readers have noticed the similarities between the psychopaths of North America and the Nazis of the nineteen thirties. This is not a coincidence, as psychopaths are all the same. They have no conscience and are concerned only with themselves. They do not hesitate to kill countless innocent people, if that will achieve the desired goal.

The only difference was the Industrial Revolution, which made possible mass murder on an industrial scale. The Nazis just took full advantage of that opportunity.

To return to the disastrous War of 1812, the spirit of Manifest Destiny refused to die.

If they could not expand north, and capture Canada, they decided to head south and west.

In 1845 the United States annexed the self-proclaimed country of Texas, even though Mexico regarded it as part of their country. The Americans looked upon Texas as a valuable addition to their country, and as it was their "Manifest Destiny" to expand from sea to sea, it was their "duty" to claim Texas as a state.

There were other rich colonies just waiting to be captured, and in 1848, the United States went to war with Mexico.

As a result of this war, other "territories" were brought into the fold. This included California, New Mexico, Arizona, Utah and Nevada. American states they may now be, but they have retained their Spanish culture and language.

Several decades later, the hostility between the northern capitalists and the southern slave owners erupted into open warfare. The capitalists were anxious to invest their capital in the southern part of the country, in order to take advantage of the abundant natural resources. The completely reactionary southern slave owners were equally determined to keep everything precisely the way it was. They wanted no part of industrial development. They were content to grow crops of cotton and tobacco, using slave labour of course.

Those two classes, capitalists and slave owners, are natural enemies. They had come together years earlier, against a common enemy, the British Empire. Yet after the war was over, the country achieved independence, and the alliance was at an end. It was just a matter of time before they went to war.

This is characteristic of the class struggle. The lesson is that our allies of today, may well become our enemies of tomorrow.

Americans went to war with themselves in the Civil War of 1861-1865. The northern part of the country, which was quite highly industrialized by that time, led by the capitalists, went to war with the completely reactionary Confederate southern states, led by the slave owners.

It is true that in the early months of the war, the south did win some impressive victories, but as most of their weapons were either made by hand or captured from the enemy, it was just a matter of time before the industrial capacity of the north swung the war in their favour. The factories of the north were able to produce vast quantities of muskets, rifles, cannon and everything else an army needs, far more than can be produced by hand, and the Confederate slave owners were over powered.

To this day, the government claims that they went to war because the states do not have the right to secede from the Union. This is an outright lie, as decades earlier, the North seceded from the United States, and was allowed to do so.

Many Americans think the country broke apart because of slavery, and that President Lincoln abolished slavery on January 1, 1863, with his now famous Emancipation Proclamation. In fact, he did nothing of the sort.

That is another lie propagated by the capitalists.

In all fairness to President Lincoln, he could not possibly have abolished slavery, if only because he did not have that authority! For that reason, if no other, to say that Lincoln "abolished slavery", is pure nonsense. After all, the Supreme Court ruled, in 1857, in the Dred Scott decision, that slavery was guaranteed in the Constitution! Only the Congress has the authority to change the Constitution! Not the president! In fact, Lincoln took the same oath all presidents take, to "preserve, protect and defend the Constitution"! In 1860, that meant defending slavery!

The Emancipation Proclamation is commonly considered the official speech, given on January 1, 1863, in which slavery was abolished in the United States. Such is hardly the case. To this day, Abraham Lincoln is honoured and respected, considered to be one of the finest presidents.

We can only stress that this speech, referred to as the Emancipation Proclamation, is not referred to as the "Abolition Proclamation". There is a good reason for this. The word "abolish" is not mentioned in the speech!

On that day, Abraham Lincoln carried through on his ultimatum, that which he had given the Confederates, in September of 1862. On that day, he gave the Confederates one hundred days to rejoin the union, or face financial ruin! He was not bluffing.

So on January 1, 1863, President Lincoln announced that the slaves, who were under the control of the Confederates, were emancipated. By the same token, the slaves who were under the control of the Union forces, were not emancipated. This is to say that the slaves in the states of Delaware, Maryland, Kentucky, Missouri and the counties of Virginia which now constitute the state of West Virginia, were not effected.

This is referred to as "selective emancipation".

This is not to say that slavery was abolished in the southern states. It was not. It just meant that the slaves who were owned by the Confederates were "emancipated".

Of course, the Confederate slave owners paid absolutely no attention to Lincoln, so the slaves in those states were not released from bondage.

We stress the fact that Lincoln merely punished the Confederates for breaking away from the Union. He did not abolish slavery, not even in the southern states. Not too surprising, as he did not have that authority!

As a result of this, almost no slaves were set free. For those people, it remained a life of bondage as usual. Most of them were probably not even aware of the fact that they had been "emancipated", and of those that were, it is doubtful that any of them even knew the meaning of the word. Slave owners are careful not to educate their slaves.

Chances are the Confederates were not even worried as they were winning some impressive victories. It took a while for the northern factories to convert to war production, and then to equip the armies of the north with modern weapons. Once this happened, the south had no chance.

It is reported that General Fremont, a Union general, was stationed in the state of Missouri, on August 30, 1861, at the start of the Civil War. He went so far as to emancipate a great many slaves, within that state. His boss, President Abraham Lincoln, was furious and ordered those slaves, those people, those human beings, returned to their rightful owners.

So much for the Great Emancipator!

General Fremont, in turn, refused to obey this outrageous order, and was fired by the president.

Not many people are prepared to risk their careers in such a manner. As for those who suggest that he was hardly one of the finest of Union generals, I can only respond that he was a man I admire. He did the right thing. Not the legal thing, but the right thing! He stood on principle.

The war gradually swung in favour of the Union, as the factories of the north began to produce vast quantities of war material. Then as the Union troops swept into the south, the slaves in those states were released from bondage. The people who formerly owned these slaves, the Confederates, also owned plantations. Without the slaves to work these plantations, these plantation owners were financially ruined, just as President Lincoln had earlier threatened.

The point is that Abraham Lincoln did not abolish slavery in the United States, not even in the southern states. That required an act of Congress. I repeat, the president does not have the authority to change the constitution!

Yet Lincoln was a true follower of Jefferson. A racist to the very core of his being. So he was able to arrange the "relocation" of many people, former slaves, who had managed to secure their freedom. As it was thought that it was too expensive to ship them to Africa, they were sent to Haiti. This was politely referred to as "colonization".

No doubt the people who were placed on board those ships thought they were going to Africa, and it was likely a dream come true. If so, then that dream soon turned into a nightmare. It is doubtful that any of them could speak French, and the people of Haiti speak only French. It is equally doubtful that any of them had any useful skills, as the slave owners were careful to train them only to grow crops, mainly cotton, and not much else. As a result of this, many of them died in Haiti.

It is reported that as many as five hundred people were sent to Haiti, as ordered by Lincoln, and if he had not been killed, a great many more could have been sent.

After the death of Lincoln, many of the survivors were returned to America.

It was not until December of 1865, almost three years after the Emancipation Proclamation, that slavery was abolished in the United States, by act of Congress, with the passage of the Thirteenth Amendment to the Constitution.

Now let us examine Canadian history. We also have a Revolutionary history, although here too, most Canadians are not aware of this.

As is well known, after Columbus stumbled upon South America in 1492, in an attempt of determine a trade route to China, the powers of Europe fought numerous battles in an attempt to seize control of the Americas. These countries included Italy, Spain, Portugal, France and Great Britain. In particular, France, Spain and Britain were each determined to gain control over North America, and fought various battles over this prize, in much the same manner as dogs fight over a bone.

Our concern is mainly that of the War of the Spanish Succession, fought between 1702 - 1713, which was primarily fought in Europe. At that time, France and Spain were allies, however temporarily. The North American theatre of war became known as "Queen Annes War", or the "French and Indian Wars", in that both sides tried to get the Native American tribes to fight for them, in return for trade goods such as muskets, gunpowder and whiskey, or as the First Nations people refer to it, "beads and trinkets".

The area in dispute included the present day Canadian Maritime provinces of Nova Scotia, New Brunswick and Prince Edward Island, at that time referred to as Acadia.

The Treaty of Utrecht, signed in 1713, officially brought an end to the war, on paper, if not in fact. The French settlers, called Acadians, were allowed to keep their land and in fact most of them retained their culture and loyalty to France. They also refused to sign an Oath of Allegiance to Britain.

As a result of this, a great many Acadians, but by no means all, were involved in various military operations against the British, helping to supply the French fortresses at Louisbourg and Fort Beausejour.

Naturally, the British commanders took a dim view of this, and in 1755 ordered the removal of the Acadians, without bothering to distinguish between those who had remained neutral and those who had resisted the occupation of Acadia.

This became known as the Expulsion of the Acadians, the Great Removal, the Great Upheaval, the Great Deportation, and in french, Le Grande Derangement.

If the British thought this would result in the destruction of the Acadians, they were mistaken. It merely spread the Acadian culture. In particular, a great many Acadians settled in the French colony of New Orleans, located in the current

American state of Louisiana. To this day, their culture remains strong.

There are certain people who are confused by this, mainly because of their accent. They now refer to themselves "Cajuns".

This is just one more example of the common history of the United States and Canada.

It was not until 1867 that four provinces came together, which is Ontario, Quebec, Nova Scotia and New Brunswick, to form the Dominion of Canada. All of these provinces had previously been under the control or influence of the French, and to this day have strong French influence. In particular, the province of Quebec remains a French country within the borders of Canada.

As soon as the new country of Canada took shape, it became anxious to expand, and of course was not terribly interested in the concerns of the French or the First Nations people.

Prince Ruperts Land was a territory in British North America consisting of the Hudson Bay drainage area, which was nominally owned by the Hudsons Bay Company, or HBC. Of course, the First Nations people who lived in the area took exception to this, properly so. In 1821, the HBC monopoly was extended to the Pacific coast. This land was not technically owned by the company, although to the people who lived there, it certainly seemed that way. The HBC "merely" had a trading monopoly enforceable on British subjects.

It was not until 1869, that the Canadian government bought the trading rights to Prince Ruperts Land from Hudsons Bay Company, and appointed an English speaking governor. This did not sit well with the settlers to the west of Ontario, that which is present day Manitoba, many of whom were French speaking Metis, where the Metis were for the most part, a mixture of French and First Nation, referred to as "Half Breeds". Many of these people served as trappers, guides and interpreters to fur traders, and also had farms. There was also an English speaking mixed race, known as Anglo Metis. To complicate matters further, there were American settlers, many of whom favoured annexing the territory to the United States.

These people with different interests amounted to a political powder keg, and the Canadian government lit the fuse by sending in people to survey the land. The Metis who owned farms, but had no title to the land, were afraid this would result in the loss of their farms. This was likely the very thing the government had planned.

The lots the Metis occupied had been laid out in the seigneurial colonial system, with long, narrow lots fronting the river, rather than the square lots favoured by the English. The Metis considered this to be a threat to their way of life, including loss of their farms, their language, religion, which was mainly Roman Catholic, and their culture. In this, they were absolutely correct.

Amid rising tensions, a leader emerged, as leaders always emerge under such conditions, and his name was Louis Riel. A Metis National Committee was formed, composed of French, Anglo and Metis delegates. This gave rise to the Red River Colony, and a Provisional Government was formed. It was rather typical, in that it was composed of people of different beliefs, ethnic backgrounds, and languages. The main thing was that they respected each other. Quite remarkably, all of the demands of the Provisional Government were agreed to, by Ottawa. These included French schools for French children, respect for the religious beliefs of all, so that they were allowed their own churches, the farmers were allowed to own the land they were tilling, and so forth.

In 1870, the Red River Colony was allowed to enter Confederation as the province of Manitoba. This is referred to as the Red River Rebellion, or First Riel Rebellion, although it was not so much a rebellion as a resistance.

Yet during the time that the Provisional Government was in power, Louis Riel had made a serious mistake. He had ordered the execution of Thomas Scott, an "Orangeman", or a Protestant, as they referred to themselves.

Scott was consumed with hatred. He hated "Indians", as well as Catholics, and especially "half breeds", as the Metis were frequently called. As Riel was all of that, he had a particular hatred for Riel, the leader of the Provisional Government. He refused to recognize the authority of that Government, and was arrested. Even though guilty of a few crimes, none of them were capital offences. Yet Riel ordered him executed, mainly because he was such a disagreeable person. This in no way changes the fact that the execution was illegal.

As a result of this, Louis Riel was banished from the country for five years.

Several years late, in the summer of 1884, in the part of the country referred to as the "North West", which now amounts to the Canadian provinces of Saskatchewan and Alberta, people were desperate. The First Nations people at least had Native rights, and were settled on Reserves, however disagreeable. By contrast, their cousins, the Metis, whom they considered poor relations, were in far worse shape. The trapping was practically a thing of the past and the bison herds, commonly called buffalo, which had previously been a main source of food and clothing, were almost wiped out. The Metis were reduced to scratching out a living on their farms.

The trouble was that the railroads were coming and settlers followed the railroads, so surveyors were first sent in to plot out square lots rather than the long, narrow lots which the Metis occupied, without actually holding title to the land. This was the very thing the Canadian government had proposed to do in Manitoba several years before, and it was Louis Riel who had managed to work out an amicable settlement.

With that in mind, the Metis, First Nations people and other settlers called upon Louis Riel to return to the North West, and lead them in their struggle with the Canadian government.

At that time, Riel was living in the United States, earning a living as a school teacher. Yet, as he was needed, he returned to Canada.

Discontent was widespread, but whereas in 1870, people in Manitoba had put aside their differences and came together, in the North West, Riel was unable to unite people.

In fact, people were rather openly questioning his sanity. It is reported that Riel had spent some time in a mental institution, which is quite reasonable, as mental illness is very real. Yet at that time, Riel was advocating war with Canada!

In the spring of 1885, in the North West, a Provisional Government was formed, and a ten point Revolutionary Bill of Rights was passed. Their demands were completely reasonable, and were presented to Ottawa. The Metis were demanding the same rights as had previously been granted to their Eastern relatives in 1870.

The response of Ottawa was something less than reasonable. The Canadian government had other ideas.

The situation had changed dramatically in fifteen years, a fact which Riel either would not or could not face. A railroad had been built, linking Ottawa with central Canada, making it much easier to move troops and equipment to the rebellious areas. The troops were referred to as the North West Mounted Police, while in fact they were more of a military force, rather than a police force. The Canadian government was feeling far more secure, less inclined to make concessions. Then too, they had not forgotten the fact that Riel had hung a man, whom he should not have hung.

Despite this, Riel decided to go to war with Canada. He chose battle, and at Duck Lake, the open rebellion was under way.

The sanity of Riel remains, to this day, a matter of debate among scholars, but his decision to go to war with the Canadian government is not in dispute. Whether or not he was personally insane, his decision was completely insane. A handful of ragtag militia, poorly armed, with almost no training, and very little equipment or provisions, and with very limited popular support, had no chance against the Canadian military.

A great many First Nation people and Metis saw the folly in this act of open warfare and refused to join the Rebellion. They just saw no point in fighting a war which they could not possibly win. The Rebellion lasted several months, and was a loose coalition of First Nation, French and Metis against the Canadian government.

Their cause was certainly just and they had every right to resist, but their tactics were faulty.

Of course the Rebellion was suppressed and the Rebels surrendered. Louis Riel and eight others were given the formality of a fair trial, before they were hung.

This caused very deep divisions within Canada, divisions which endure to this day. The French think Riel was hung mainly because he was French, and the French are treated as second class citizens.

The French are not the only Canadian citizens who have legitimate grievances.

The Canadian government made every effort to wipe out the First Nations culture. In particular, deep divisions were caused with the Indian Act of 1876, in which First Nation children were required to attend school. This gave rise to the nightmare of Indian Residential Schools, which were boarding schools for First Nations, Metis, and Inuit children, although at that time the Inuit were referred to as Eskimos.

At the age of six, children were apprehended and taken to boarding schools and assimilated into Canadian culture. They were not allowed to speak their own language, even if that language was French. They had to speak English. The teachers were bilingual, and they wanted to speak to each other in French, without having the children understand what was being said. In addition, there were numerous examples of physical and sexual abuse. Corporal punishment, in the form of beatings, was justified as the only way of "saving souls", in order to "civilize the savage", or as punishment for running away. A great many of them died in those schools. The last Residential School closed in 1996.

The goal of these schools has been described as "cultural genocide".

Also under the Indian Act, in 1884 the First Nations people were forbidden to assemble. Their traditional potlatches, or powwows, were banned, at least until 1951.

Of course, the people continued to gather and celebrate, to have their potlatches, to celebrate their culture, but in secret.

In the twentieth century, the mistreatment of the First Nations people continued.

A decision was made, in the province of British Columbia, to place a dam at Hudson Hope and flood a significant part of the Rocky Mountain Trench, in the interests of generating electricity. The government reasoned that the area was practically devoid of people, and this was a fine way to generate some money.

The key word here is "practically". In fact, there were a number of people living in the area to be flooded, but as they were First Nations, the government chose to disregard them.

In the nineteen sixties, these people, the Dene, were not completely settled down on Reserves, and continued to live a somewhat nomadic existence, wandering around, spending a great deal of time on their "trap lines", as they referred to them. The government gave them a Reserve, called Fort Graham, but much to the fury of government officials, they spent little time on the Reserve. On the other hand, the Canadian government decided to "relocate" them, so this lack of occupancy worked in favour of the government.

In all fairness, it is not clear whether it was the federal government or the provincial government, or both, which was involved in this forced removal.

It was probably in the year 1969 that all the cabins on the Reserve of Fort Graham were torched, just as the dam was going in place at Hudson Hope, and Williston Lake was forming.

The people who lived in Fort Graham owned very little, just a few things which most of us consider the necessities of life, such as shelter, clothes, bedding, winter boots, dishes, pots and pans, and such.

After their homes were burned, the people were left with the clothes they were wearing, and winter was fast approaching.

They were advised, by government officials, that they had to move to a different location, to a place called Parsnip, which is little better than a gravel pit, where there were houses waiting for them.

The people were divided, so that some of them moved to Parsnip, and sure enough, there were the houses, prefabricated pieces of garbage, mobile homes which were designed with California weather in mind. As soon as the temperature dropped, the water pipes froze, and it was almost impossible to keep those homes heated. They missed their log cabins, which may not have been pretty, but they were warm.

Yet there were a few people who refused to move to Parsnip and, with the water rising quickly, jumped in river boats and made their way up river to Ingenika Point. This was an extremely dangerous trip, as the rising water forced trees, and sometimes whole groups of trees, to pop to the surface. In addition, the trees which had already floated to the surface frequently blocked the channel, or the lake, as it was forming. Sometimes the only way forward was to stand in the front of the boat, with a chain saw, and cut the way through. It was a tedious, slow, dangerous process, but they finally made it to the relative safety of the Point, above the level of the rising water. Then it was a little matter of cutting down trees and building some log cabins, and quickly, as it was fall and winter was almost upon them. By working together, they succeeded, shared the little they had, and managed to survive the winter.

The government response to the people who had refused their generous offer of hospitality at Parsnip, was to cut them off all social assistance. As they had no food, little clothing and few tools, the government clearly expected them to freeze or starve that first winter. The government under estimated the Dene.

Late in the fall, one of their relatives from town arrived with a riverboat full of groceries, and dropped it off for them, with the understanding that they could pay for it later. This helped get them through that first winter, as the groceries were rationed, but late in the winter, they still ran out. At one point, they were reduced to eating nothing but cranberries, which stay on the bushes all winter.

With the arrival of the spring thaw, the boys shot beaver and snared rainbow trout, and the people ate beaver meat and fish.

It should be noted that just before the onset of winter, the big game outfitter in the area had placed the equipment he had not used in a cache, safe from bears. This included a considerable amount of food, in the form of rice, flour, sugar, coffee, tea, macaroni and spaghetti, among other things. When that outfitter arrived back in the spring, to find the people still alive but desperately hungry, he was surprised to find that his food cache was exactly as he had left it. Even facing starvation, they had resisted the temptation to steal.

During that first terrible winter, one of the girls had been badly injured. A rifle accidentally fired and hit her in the elbow. Her relatives managed somehow to get to a two-way radio and call for medical assistance. The government responded by telling them to "bring her to town". Even though this was not possible, the government refused to send help, at least not until the spring. By that time, she had recovered, by the Grace of God and the nursing of the other girls.

The boys spent the first winter trapping and managed to earn enough money to pay for the supplies which had been dropped off the previous fall.

It is not clear which government agencies were involved in this "relocation", although it was probably a group effort. It is clear that the torching of the cabins on the Reserve was an act of arson, and further, no one has ever been charged with that crime. No doubt other crimes were committed, such as cutting those people off of social assistance and placing their lives in danger by flooding the land. As yet, no one has been held accountable for their actions.

Perhaps those people think that the First Nations people, are outside the protection of the law.

CHAPTER 9
911 and Guantanamo Bay

The events of September 11, 2001, are well known to all of us, or at least all Americans.

This day is generally referred to as nine eleven, or 911. All of us were completely shocked on that day, and it has been compared to the day on which President Kennedy was shot. The event was so shocking that we all remember precisely the day and exactly what we were doing when we learned about it.

This is not to say that we know exactly what happened on that fateful day. Certain facts we know and there are other theories which are presented as facts, but are distortions and outright lies. This is not too surprising, as the government officials are habitual liars.

The facts, which are not in dispute, are that two huge airlines crashed into the Twin Towers, the first at 8:46 into the North Tower of the World Trade Center, and the second plane crashed into the South Tower of the World Trade Center, at 9:03.

It is also a fact that there was an explosion at the Pentagon at 9:37, which caused major damage to that building.

Further, the south tower collapsed at 9:59 after burning for 55 minutes, while the North Tower collapsed at 10:28 after burning for 102 minutes. Also, World Trade Center 7, or WTC7, a 47 story skyscraper, also caught fire and collapsed at 5:21 pm.

We stress that these facts are beyond dispute, as we have pictures, videos and eye witness accounts.

This atrocity resulted in the deaths of thousands of innocent people.

The government has blamed this butchery on al-qaeda and Osama bin Laden.

They would have us believe that an individual, hiding in a cave half a world away, could organize the hand picking of twenty suicide bombers, smuggle them into the United States, train several of them once in the country to fly planes, and not just small planes but commercial aircraft, then take over four huge aircraft and fly them into buildings.

Assuming this is true, it is an absolutely incredible accomplishment. To think that such an individual could outsmart every American government intelligence agency in the country! This is not likely, although the government would have us believe it to be true. If it is true, then those intelligence agencies are completely incompetent.

Nonsense! No one, or at least no one in his right mind, has ever accused the American government intelligence agencies of being incompetent. In fact, they are among the finest intelligence agencies in the world. Nothing of any importance gets past them. The events of 911 did not happen despite the efforts of these fine intelligence agencies, but *because* of these agencies.

The official government version of events, is that on that fateful day,19 suicide bombers hid metal weapons either on their persons or in carry-on luggage, passed through metal detectors at the airport, without the metal being detected, and made their way onto four commercial airlines. Then they used these weapons to overpower the crew and passengers of those airplanes, and the suicide bombers who had been trained to fly were able to take control of those huge aircraft and fly them, with great precision, into the Twin Towers and the Pentagon. A fourth jet crashed into Pennsylvania.

As anyone who has ever travelled on a commercial aircraft can testify, it is simply not possible to pass through airline security with metal weapons. The metal detectors do a fine job of detecting metal, and the security personnel are highly trained.

Further, they tell us that the aviation fuel from the jets which hit the Twin Tower burned so hot that it melted the steel girders, which caused the skyscrapers to collapse. Not only that, but the fires from the Twin Towers spread to World Trade Center 7, or WTC7, and those fires also burned so hot that the steel girders on that building also melted.

The trouble is that the physical evidence does not support this explanation.

To determine the truth, we have only to start with the rubble of WTC7.

The fact of the matter is that all sky scrapers are equipped with sprinkler systems. It is the law. As soon as the heat sensors detect excessive heat, then the sprinklers are activated, and the area is saturated with water.

The fires at WTC7 were small and isolated. As that is the case, the sprinklers should have been activated, and those small fires should have been extinguished. That never happened. How is it that the sprinklers on WTC7 failed to work? The only explanation is that the sprinklers were disabled.

As a result of this, the fires were able to burn, but of course they did not burn nearly as hot as the fires in the Twin Towers. Yet the official government explanation, is that these small, isolated fires, brought down this sky scraper, WTC7! Nonsense!

Various eye witnesses have testified to the fact that melted steel beams were found in the rubble of WTC7. Is it possible that the fires, which were clearly seen on video, on several floors of WTC7, were hot enough to melt steel beams?

The New York Times quoted Dr. Jonathan Barnett, professor of fire protection engineering at Worcester Polytechnic Institute, as saying that fire in WTC7 "would not explain steel members in the debris pile that appear to have been partly evaporated in extraordinarily high temperatures. Building fires do not melt steel structural element for two reasons. First, the temperatures are not high enough. It is hard to get a fire hot enough to melt steel... Second, and perhaps more important, steel is a great conductor of heat. When you heat part of a steel structure (and remember the fires in WTC7 were, by all accounts, small and isolated) the heat is conducted away from the point where the fire is applied, cooling it." (parenthesis by Dr. Barnett)

It is the opinion of this world renowned expert that the fires in WTC7 could not possibly have caused the collapse of the building, so something else must have melted those steel beams.

This begs the question, just what could create those high temperatures?

The answer is explosives. One of the few products which can generate such high heat under such conditions is thermite, a chemical compound used in demolition explosives.

The fact is that WTC7 was set up for demolition, by explosive experts, using thermite, long before the two aircraft crashed into the Twin Towers. Those same experts disabled the sprinkler system on WTC7.

Now let us examine the explanation that the gasoline from the planes which crashed into the Twin Towers caused fires which burned so hot that they melted the steel girders that supported those skyscrapers.

The trouble is that such steel melts at 2800 degrees Fahrenheit or 1535 degrees Celcius. Further, it has been calculated that if each plane had 10,000 gallons of fuel, and if allowed to burn under ideal conditions, then the temperatures reached could at most be 536 degrees Fahrenheit or 280 degrees Celsius. That temperature is far below the temperatures needed to melt steel girders!

Of course, the conditions that fateful day were absolutely not ideal, so that the temperatures reached were no where near as high. At best, the structural strength of the steel beams was reduced by less than one percent, which is insignificant.

There is absolutely no way that the burning of the fuel from the two planes which struck the Twin Towers caused the collapse of the Twin Towers. The temperatures reached were no where near hot enough to weaken the steel beams, not to mention melting them. Yet the steel beams on the Twin Towers were also melted, and again we must conclude that thermite was used.

This brings us to the explosion at the Pentagon. Without doubt, this explosion happened, as there are numerous eye witnesses who heard the sound. The damage to the Pentagon has also been well established through eye witness account, pictures and videos.

Now let us consider the government claim that the huge aircraft approached the Pentagon at very low altitude, flying directly over countless residential houses.

If this were true, no doubt people would have noticed. No one noticed a giant aircraft flying directly overhead for the very fine and simple reason that it never happened.

To this day the government also claims that the airline crashed into the Pentagon and burst into flames, creating an inferno so intense that the aircraft and all its parts were completely incinerated, to the point where nothing is left. More nonsense!

From the pictures of the site of the explosion at the Pentagon, it is clear that there is no tail section of the aircraft, protruding from the building. Further, there is no sight of engines, luggage, seats or bodies of the passengers and crew. There is no indication of the landing gear scraping the ground, as the aircraft approached the building.

That plane, which supposedly hit the pentagon, is a 757, which, in imperial units, is 155 feet long, has a wing span of 125 feet, and over 44 feet tall at the tail.

At the point of impact, the hole is only 20 feet in diameter and just a few feet off the ground. The idea that an aircraft, 125 feet wide, could crash into a building, creating a hole of a mere 20 feet, is utterly ridiculous.

As we have already determined, the fire created by the combustion of gasoline is no where near hot enough to completely incinerate a plane and all its parts, not to mention human remains. The reason that no parts of the plane were seen at the Pentagon, is the same reason that no one saw the huge plane fly directly over their houses, just as no one saw the smoke and fire from the explosion of the plane. There was no plane! There was no smoke and fire!

To suggest that a plane struck the Pentagon is the very height of absurdity. Of all the government explanations concerning the events of 911, this is the most ridiculous.

Without doubt, the explosion at the Pentagon was not caused by an aircraft, so just what did cause that explosion?

The answer is almost certainly a cruise missile. The American military fired a cruise missile into their own headquarters!

This brings us to the mysterious fourth plane which was supposedly hijacked.

It is possible that this plane did exist and was shot down over Pennsylvania. If that is the case, then it was very likely shot down by an F16 American fighter plane.

So now we can piece together the events of that fateful day. It was clearly an act of terror, mass murder, a crime against humanity, but foreign terrorists were not responsible. In fact, it is doubtful that Osama bin Laden ever existed.

American terrorists were responsible for this elaborate act of mass murder!

No doubt for weeks before that fateful day, demolition experts were busy setting thermite explosives in the Twin Towers and WTC7. Two commercial size jets were set to fly by remote control, without passengers or crew, of course. A cruise missile was set to be fired into the Pentagon, and possibly a fighter jet was set to shoot down a commercial aircraft.

Without doubt, a great many people were involved in the conspiracy to commit this act of mass murder.

Despite this, we are well aware that something caused fires to burn so hot that the steel girders were melted, so that the buildings collapsed. It has been reported that even 21 days after the attack, the fires were still burning and the molten steel was still running.

From this we can conclude that explosives charges were placed in WTC7 as well as the Twin Towers, long before the planes struck the buildings. The sprinkler system in WTC7 was also disabled and very likely, it was arranged for various fires to ignite in WTC7. It was then a simple matter of guiding the two planes, by remote control, into the Twin Towers. It is very likely that no one was in those planes. After all, we have only the word of government officials that the planes were occupied.

This raises the question, why would Americans want to kill Americans?

In order to answer that question, we will once again refer to the Marxism.

At the end of the nineteenth century, capitalism reached the monopoly stage, just as Marx predicted it would. This gave birth to that stage of capitalism which is referred to as imperialism. As Lenin points out in his book, Imperialism, the Highest Stage of Capitalism :

"Imperialism is capitalism in that stage of development in which the domination of monopolies and finance capital has established itself; in which the export of capital has acquired pronounced importance; in which the division of the world among the international trusts has begun; in which the partition of all the territories of the globe among the great capitalist powers has been completed."

As the title of the book suggests, imperialism is the age of monopoly capitalism and it is capitalism at its highest, most rotten stage. The capitalists who embrace imperialism are completely reactionary, and it is characteristic of such people that they love war. It is their nature. War gives rise to huge profits, as a result of factories producing an abundance of goods, which are almost immediately destroyed, creating the need for ever more goods. The only disadvantage is that people end up getting killed and the suffering of civilians is intense, but as the imperialists are all psychopaths, this is a matter of complete indifference. The only thing which matters to them is their profit.

With that in mind, it is best to bear in mind that at the dawn of the age of imperialism, the American capitalists embraced imperialism. As the lickspittle bourgeois historians phrase it, America "became a world power" at that time.

In fact, the American capitalists, the bourgeoisie, decided to go into competition with the other "great powers" in an attempt to rule the world, to take control of as many colonies as possible.

It was somewhat late in the game that the American imperialists decided to try their hand at ruling the world, as the world was almost completely divided up between highly industrialized imperialist countries, such as Britain, France, Spain, Japan and Germany. The only way to proceed was to steal some colonies from other imperialists.

It should be noted that this is the characteristic response of imperialists generally. They are constantly probing for weakness, anxious to steal anything they can from whomever they can.

The American imperialists noticed that Spain was perhaps the weakest of the imperialist countries, and decided to challenge that country for control of the colonies of Cuba and the Philippines. The trouble was that the American public, the working people, the common people, as we call ourselves, were no different from the working people of any other country. We just want to live a life of peace, work and pay taxes, raise our children and so forth. None of us wants war, especially not a war with someone with whom we have no quarrel.

On the other hand, if we are attacked, we are quite fully prepared to defend ourselves.

The imperialists are well aware of this, and have a history of fabricating incidents of attacks on American citizens, in order to whip up sentiment in favour of war.

With that in mind, the imperialists took the bull by the horns and sent an American battleship, the Maine, to Cuba, in 1898. The ship was moored in Havana harbour when it exploded and sank, with great loss of American life. This explosion was almost certainly caused by members of the American military.

Of course, the Spanish were blamed for the attack, and American "public opinion" rapidly changed. Almost overnight, the American public was in favour of war. The imperialists promptly went to war with Spain. The factories were producing, the goods produced were promptly destroyed, creating a need for more goods, the profits of the capitalists sky rocketed, and Cuba and the Philippines became American colonies. Mission accomplished.

Several years later, in 1914, the imperialists were anxious to enter the carnage which was devastating Europe, but at that time the American public was again anxious to remain neutral.

In response, the American government provoked the German navy by sending ships, especially passenger ships, into waters which were patrolled by German submarines.

They also let it be known that these ships were carrying war material for Britain, which made them legitimate targets for German submarines.

As a result of this, the luxury cruise liner Lusitania was sunk with great loss of life.

Public opinion gradually turned against neutrality and in 1917, the United States was finally able to declare war on Germany. The imperialists were once again in their glory, which is to say, they were at war.

After the "Great War", or the First World War, there was once again a period of peace, but then war once again erupted in Europe. But then again the American public was in favour of neutrality. They wanted no part of European war. The imperialists wanted every part of European war. Try as they might to provoke Germany into declaring war, it was not working.

The imperialists are resourceful people, and as the direct approach was not working, they decided on the indirect approach.

The Pacific fleet in San Diego was dispatched to Pearl Harbour in Hawaii. It was thought, correctly, that the Japanese could not resist such a temptation. The Japanese took the bait, and in 1941, the fleet was destroyed. Almost overnight, the American public was screaming for war. The icing on the cake was the fact that Germany also declared war on the United States, which was precisely what the Americans wanted. The war with Japan was a side issue, something of a bonus.

At the end of World War 2, there was a brief interlude of peace, followed by a war with Korea, as part of the United Nations effort, led by the United States, to prop up the southern part of the country.

As far as the imperialists were concerned, it was brief, but nice while it lasted, and sadly, did not spread to war with China and the Soviet Union.

It should be noted that at that time, both the Soviet Union and China were Socialist countries, which gave the imperialists another reason to go to war with them. Destroying a truly Socialist country is their idea of "containing the spread of Communism", as they phrase it.

Those two countries are absolutely not Socialist now, as the bourgeoisie of both countries have succeeded in restoring capitalism in those countries. Temporarily, of course.

Opportunities for more war soon presented themselves. In Indochina, the Vietnamese in particular were kicking out their colonial occupiers, first the Japanese and then the French. So of course the American imperialists were anxious to fill the void. They were determined to pick up where the French left off, and they did.

Starting in 1961, American troops were sent to Viet Nam, but only as "advisors", and the government was anxious to send in huge numbers of troops and have a proper war.

They were determined to find an excuse to allow President Johnson to send vast numbers of troops into Vietnam, which he most certainly did.

The trouble was that the public was once again opposed to the war. It was once again time for the American forces to be attacked. The dastardly North Vietnamese did just that. This attack became known as the Gulf of Tonkin incident. It was reported that an American destroyer was attacked by North Vietnamese torpedo boats, in 1964. The "Gulf of Tonkin" incident gave President Johnson the excuse he needed to send in half a million men.

Of course, no one was hurt in this "incident" and in fact this became an embarrassment for the American imperialists years later, when they were forced to admit that the attack never happened.

From 1964 to 1975, tens of thousands of American young men, the finest of the country, were killed there. Countless others were wounded, physically and mentally, and after they returned home, many committed suicide. The American people were absolutely opposed to any more foreign wars. It is against this background that we must consider the events of 911.

At that time, it was clear to the imperialists that this public sentiment against war had to change. They knew that something drastic had to be done, and as they had learned from the experience of the Gulf of Tonkin incident, such fabrications were not sufficient. The country had to come under attack, a great many people had to die, and this incident had to be as shocking as the Japanese attack on Pearl Harbour. Even better, the people who were to be sacrificed had to be innocent civilians.

As there are no enemies who are stupid enough to attempt such an attack, the government agencies decided to resort to terrorism themselves, and blame it on someone else.

September 11, 2001, was carefully planned and executed, and supremely successful.

As a result of this, the American public was outraged and the country immediately went to war, first with Iraq and then with Afghanistan. Of course, neither country had anything to do with the events of 911, but that was of no concern to the imperialists. The country was once again at war, and the capitalists were making a huge profit. Mission accomplished.

The fact is that a great many people were involved in the conspiracy which is generally referred to as 911. All of them are Americans, terrorists and psychopaths one and all. We should mention that a psychopath is an individual who completely lacks a conscience, someone who cares only for himself. For those who seek justice, there is no need to travel halfway around the world to root these people out. They are right here in North America, hiding in plain sight.

There are a great many of them and the fact is that a chain is only as strong as its weakest link. All it takes is for one of them to break his or her silence, and the truth will emerge. As those people have no sense of morality, it follows that they also have no sense of loyalty. They are concerned only with themselves and will not hesitate to inform on their former associates. Whatever it takes to save themselves!

It is important to bear in mind that it was members of a different class, the capitalist class, the bourgeoisie, who are responsible for this act of mass murder, this atrocity. If nothing else, this alone should serve to remove any lingering doubts any members of the working class has, as to the differences which we have with the capitalists, the bourgeoisie. Our differences cannot be peacefully reconciled. There cannot possibly be any peaceful transition to socialism, at least not in America. The bourgeoisie have shown their true colours, and this proves, beyond any shadow of a doubt, that they, the bourgeoisie, will do whatever it takes to maintain their power and wealth.

It has been suggested that the International Criminal Court, the ICC, may have to be brought in, as the government will not prosecute themselves. This is not about to happen, for a number of reasons. For one thing, the ICC has what is called "complementary jurisdiction", which means that it is prepared to step in only when a national court is unable or unwilling to do so.

Also, it has jurisdiction for crimes in countries that are signatories of the Rome Statute that established the ICC. The United States did not sign that statute, and does not recognize the authority of the ICC. However, if members of the American government were to commit crimes in a country which does recognize the ICC, then conceivably such individuals could be charged. Such a country would first have to refer the matter to the ICC, and then it is up to the ICC to determine if there is grounds to charge those people with war crimes or crimes against humanity. Then again, the United Nations Security Council could refer a case to the ICC, but given that the US has a veto in that body, that is not about to happen.

As for trying people in absence, that too is something the ICC does not.

No, these mass murderers, these people who are guilty of crimes against humanity, are our problem, and we are going to have to deal with them, after the Revolution, of course. Working people are not sentimental souls, prone to legal nit picking, and those who are accused will not be allowed to hide behind a battery of high priced lawyers. They will be brought to justice, have to face a working class court, possibly a tribunal, and they will in turn be held accountable for their actions. Before the working class is through with them, they will likely wish they had been brought before the ICC!

It is entirely possible that those who are convicted of mass murder will receive the death penalty. Such psychopaths deserve nothing less.

They are not the only ones who are likely to face working class justice.

As is well known, the US has a prison located in Guantanamo Bay in Cuba, also known as Gitmo. They do not call it a prison, they call it a "detention centre", and the prisoners are called "detainees". As if changing the name changes the nature of the beast!

The government hired several legal advisors to tell them precisely what they wanted to hear, and of course, those legal eagles did just that. The government officials were advised that Guantanamo prison was outside US legal jurisdiction, and as such, the prisoners were not entitled to any of the protections of the Geneva Convention. Accordingly, people are held without charges, without legal council, and are in fact tortured. Not that the officials call it torture. They call it "Enhanced Interrogation Techniques", or EIT. They have once again changed the name, in an attempt to cover up the crime.

Amnesty International has referred to it as the Gulag of our time, a human rights scandal, and the United Nations has called for it to be closed. Even American officials have conceded that prisoners have been tortured, by means of sleep deprivation, beatings, stress positions, sexual degradation and water boarding. As anyone who has been subjected to water boarding can testify, it is definitely a form of torture. Such people, under the torture of water boarding, are prepared to confess to the assassination of Kennedy!

With that in mind, the people who engage in these acts of torture are not only breaking the law, they are also acting in a manner which is supremely stupid. The information extracted from people in this manner is completely unreliable. Such people will say anything, in an attempt to relieve the pain. Who can blame them?

The people who are responsible for this prison, those who give the orders, as well as the guards who carry out those orders, will also be held accountable. It was established many years ago, at the Nuremberg trials, that "following orders", is not a legal defence.

There is also the not so little matter of the invasion of Iraq and Afghanistan, as well as the firing of cruise missiles into several countries, killing a great many civilians. The people responsible for these acts of murder will also be facing justice, after the Revolution.

CHAPTER 10
What To Expect?

The Occupy Movement has not so much died down, as morphed into a Revolutionary Movement, and has spread around the world. We can think of it as the granddaddy of all revolutions. It is not confined to one country or even one part of the world. Those who are taking part in this Revolution must support workers in other parts of the world. They are our Brothers and Sisters, our Comrades.

Those who have read this book from the beginning are well aware that I have consistently explained the scientific terms and repeated the common words along with the scientific terms. There are some readers who find this very tiresome, and perhaps it is. So many of our Comrades are common people, those who just recently became politically active. I am mainly concerned with them. They must be "brought up to speed"!The importance of learning these scientific terms must be stressed.

As for those who think that I am overstating the case, may I suggest you consider the American Confederacy of the nineteenth century. The Confederate slave owners were well aware of the power of knowledge, at least in the hands of their slaves. They went to considerable length to ensure that their slaves remained as clueless as possible, unable to read, count, and even unaware of the four directions, north, south, east and west. This helped ensure that the slaves were in no condition to rebel or even make a run for their freedom.

The situation of today is somewhat different, but only to a degree. We, the working class, the proletariat, are wage slaves. We sell ourselves by the hour, of necessity, as we have no choice in the matter. It is the only way in which we can survive. The capitalists pay us, by the hour, and work us as hard as possible, while paying us as little as possible. The capitalists are members of a different class, the bourgeoisie, and they are well aware of that which they are doing. They are supremely well educated. It suits their purposes just fine to keep us, the working class, completely unaware of ourselves as a class.

At present, strictly speaking, this Movement is not a truly Revolutionary Movement, as the working class is not aware of itself as a class. It remains a Movement striving for economic and political reform, and it may well win a few paltry reforms, but nothing of any substance, nothing which is not acceptable to the bourgeoisie. They in turn will continue to crush and exploit us, the working class, the Proletariat, becoming ever more wealthy, in the process.

The intellectuals, those who have considerable education, must play the role of "Navigator", to provide the direction to the working class, based on the Revolutionary Theories of Marx and Lenin. Or "remove the blindfold", if you prefer that metaphor.

Regardless of the metaphor, it is necessary to bring to the working class the awareness of itself as a class, of the necessity of Revolution, of Council Power and the subsequent Dictatorship of the Proletariat.

The existence of classes must be stressed. There are occasions when it is necessary and sufficient to over simplify, especially when communicating with the much less advanced. In such cases, explain to working people, the members of the public, that they are "wage slaves", Proletarians. Further, explain that it is the members of the capitalist class, the billionaires, the bourgeoisie, who own the banks and corporations, and in fact anything of any considerable value. Their only concern is with making a profit, and they make a profit from those of us who work for them. Further, the harder they work us and the less they pay us, the higher the profit. It is not by chance that their profits are huge. They work us as hard as possible, while paying us as little as possible.

This enables them to live a life of luxury and we, in turn, live in poverty.

That is the way the system is set up now, but that is not the way it has to be.

Instead of having the factories and mills and such, run for a profit, strictly for the benefit of the billionaires, why not have them run for the benefit of everyone, the majority of the people, the working class, the Proletariat?

The answer to that question is that it would never occur to the capitalists, the bourgeoisie, to work for the common good. Such a thought has never crossed their minds! They are strictly one way, their way, the way of profit, the way of putting money in their pockets. As long as the billionaires, the bourgeoisie, are in charge, that will not change.

Yet after the revolution, after we establish the Dictatorship of the Proletariat, we will have to face the fact that we still need certain capitalists, or at least those who served the capitalists so well, under capitalism. These "intellectuals and salaried personnel" are highly skilled, well educated people, scientists and engineers, among other things. Planning and organizing production, on a nationwide scale, are examples of such skills. That is simply beyond the ability of most workers.

These professional people served the capitalists well, under capitalism, and will serve the working class even better, under socialism. We are determined to offer them the respect they deserve, as well as the wages. They, in turn, will help to train select working class people.

As for those who dispute that statement, thinking that perhaps these professional people will be reluctant to assist in building socialism, may I suggest that when faced with the alternative, they will be only too anxious to cooperate!

It is one thing to overthrow the capitalists, to smash the existing state apparatus, and establish the Dictatorship of the Proletariat. It is something else entirely to get the economy running smoothly. That requires the assistance of certain specialists. As they are highly skilled, it is only right that they should be well paid.

It is hoped that this little chip of a book may be of some limited usefulness. For those who have just recently become politically active, it is hoped that these scientific terms make sense.

We have got to quit regarding the billionaires as people, just like ourselves, who have children whom they love very much, just as we love our children.

While it is true that they love their children, that in no way changes the fact that they are the enemy. They are quite prepared to allow us and our children to starve, if that is what it takes to increase their profit.

We must face the fact that the billionaires, the bourgeoisie, are completely reactionary. As such, we can expect absolutely nothing progressive from them. They will stoop to any depth to maintain their power and wealth, and will make every effort to divert the Revolutionary Movement.

It is true that they are in a severe jam financially, with various countries of the world on the verge of bankruptcy. Global economic collapse is threatened. This is not to say that they will collapse under their own weight. They will not. As reactionaries, they have got to be destroyed. We cannot just sit back and wait for them to collapse, as that will not happen.

We must put aside any differences we may have, just as the American Revolutionaries did in 1776, just as the Revolutionary people of Manitoba did in 1870.

At that time, people of various ethnic backgrounds, languages, religions and beliefs put aside those differences and came together to form a government. They respected the beliefs of each other. We do not have to share the beliefs of each other, and in fact we do not have to love each other, but we absolutely must respect each other.

In North America now, we have people who speak French, Spanish, English, Italian and numerous other languages. We also have First Nations, Afro American, Caucasian, Asian descent, as well as LGBT, which stands for lesbian, gay, bisexual, and transgender, young and old, employed, unemployed and under employed, students, teachers, lawyers, doctors, nurses, drivers, technicians, engineers, retired people and war veterans. We are all part of the working class, and we must stand together, as we all have a common enemy, the capitalists, the bourgeoisie, the billionaires.

As the Revolution gains strength and the empires collapse, we can expect nations to declare independence. We must support them in their quest for national liberation.

Here in Canada, we can expect Quebec to achieve independence, form a separate republic and separate from Canada. We must support the people of Quebec in this effort.

It is clear that the American Empire is on the verge of collapse. Three separate independent socialist republics have already taken shape. One is on the east coast, one is on the west coast, and one is in the industrial heartland of the midwest.

On the east coast, the New England states first split in two. This makes complete sense, as the three northern states of Maine, New Hampshire and Vermont are quite rural, while the three southern states of Massachusetts, Connecticut and Rhode Island are quite urban.

The three southern states have joined up with the states of New York, New Jersey, Delaware and Pennsylvania.

On the west coast, the three states of California, Washington and Oregon have also come together.

In the midwest, the seven states of Ohio, Michigan, Illinois, Indiana, Kentucky, Minnesota and Wisconsin are now united.

Incidentally, the population of these three areas, soon to be republics, consist of approximately half the population of America.

The formation of these three areas, soon to become independent socialist republics, can be explained only by the fact that Workers Councils have taken shape, within those areas. These Councils, within certain states, then decided to unite, as they had a great deal in common. We can expect the Workers Councils of other states to follow suit.

These Worker Councils are keeping a "low profile", with good reason! The Capitol Hill Autonomous Zone, within the city of Seattle, was effectively a Commune, created by a Workers Council. The American government was quick to crush that Zone, with considerable brutality! Alone, it stood no chance!

Now these Workers Councils are preparing for the Revolution. They know what to expect. For that reason, they are arming, equipping and training a great many workers. As I have covered this in another article, there is no need to repeat it here.

I can only stress that at the time the republics declare independence, we can expect the "social chauvinist", including those who claim to be followers of Marx and Lenin, to attempt to take over the existing state apparatus, and use it for their own purposes. In other words, set themselves up as the new rulers! The existing state apparatus must be destroyed! Council Power! The Dictatorship of the Proletariat!

That leaves numerous other states. It is reasonable to assume that most of them will follow suit.

As previously mentioned, the state of Texas was, at one time, a self-described republic. It could well choose to once again form a republic.

Some of the states which formed the Confederacy may once again form a republic, only this time an "Afro American" or "Black" Republic.

The southwest part of the country was taken from Mexico, yet the people have managed to maintain their Spanish heritage. No doubt they too will separate, and form a republic, or perhaps rejoin Mexico.

The southern midwest was purchased from France, and to this day, maintains a considerable French influence, especially among the Cajuns. It is reasonable to expect them also to go their own way, possibly linking up with Quebec.

Alaska and Hawaii have been granted the status of states, even though they are mere colonies. No doubt, they too will separate, forming separate republics.

It is not well known that America "owns" sixteen "Territories", another name for colonies. Five of these are classified as "Protectorates", and the "permanent residents" of four of these "Protectorates", have been granted the status of American citizens.

The people of Puerto Rico, Guam, United States Virgin Islands and Northern Marianas, are American citizens by birth. Citizens "in name only", I might add! The people of American Samoa are classified as "Nationals", so that they can take up residence in America, and apply for citizenship.

The status of the people who live in the other eleven "Protectorates" is not clear.

Incidentally, these terms are not mine. It is clear that all are colonies. It is also clear that the people who live in those "Territories" have every reason to feel bitter. No doubt all will soon declare independence.

At present, the revolutionary motion is not class conscious. There are posters and slogans, but none of them make any reference to classes. Everything that is being protested is acceptable to the capitalists, the bourgeoisie. This must change.

We will know that we are raising the consciousness of the working class when the posters and banners proclaim, in the finest tradition of Marx and Engels:

SCIENTIFIC SOCIALISM!

DICTATORSHIP OF THE PROLETARIAT!

WORKERS OF THE WORLD, UNITE!

Council Power!

www.ingramcontent.com/pod-product-compliance
Lightning Source LLC
Chambersburg PA
CBHW032057020426
42335CB00011B/387